BARBARA
O'NEILL

Self heal *by design*

The role of microorganisms in healing

REVISED 2024 UK EDITION

This book is dedicated to the Creator of this amazing body with its fine and detailed system of healing and restoration.

Barbara O'Neill, 1800 Nulla Nulla Creek Road,
Bellbrook, NSW 2440, Australia

www.barbhealth.com

The information in this book is not intended as a substitute for consulting with your physician or other healthcare provider. The publisher and author are not responsible for any adverse effects of consequences resulting from the use of any suggestions, preparations or procedures contained in this book. All matters relating to your health should be discussed with your doctor.

Scripture quotations from The King James Bible.

ISBN 978-0-6486118-1-3

This book was

Proofread by Lindy Schneider

Designed by Shane Winfield/Advent Design

Cover photo by Masterfile / Shane Winfield

Illustrations by Masterfile / Andrew Genn, iStockphoto.com

Recipe photos by:

Adobe Stock—page 130.
Dreamstime.com—pages, 135.
Masterfile.com—pages 117, 132, 148.
iStockphoto.com—page 129, 138, 143, 147, 150.

Typeset 9.5/14 Milo Serif

Special thanks to Emma Loberg, Jessica Pickering,
Michaela O'Neil and Patsy Scott

Printed in the United Kingdom

Contents

—CHAPTER ONE—

Sickness is No Accident

The body has a plan

"It is highly dishonourable for a reasonable soul, living in so divinely a built mansion as the body she resides in, to be totally unacquainted with its exquisite structure."
— Robert Boyle, 1690

The human body is the exquisite structure in which we each reside, and surely it is the responsibility of every human being to know something about the house we live in. Allow me the pleasure of assisting you to become acquainted with your exquisite structure.

The human body has the ability to heal itself. It is a self-healing organism.

The question is then posed: "If this is so, why are so many sick?" The human body *will* heal itself *if* given the right conditions. Unfortunately, many today are ignorant of these conditions.

The aim of this book is to explore the answer to this great question that billions of dollars in medical expenditure are not solving.

We can understand how cars, aeroplanes, computers and machinery work, and treat them with the respect they require in order to keep them operating in optimum condition. When it comes to the amazing organism in which we reside, we have to conclude that for the majority, there is an astounding lack of any real knowledge of the working and care that is required to keep it in a condition to carry us smoothly and trouble-free through this great journey of life.

Let's start with the bare basics—the cycle of life. All living things eventually die and are returned back to dust.

How does this relate to sickness in the human body? As we will soon see it has everything to do with it, for this cycle of life is happening in a living breathing body. It is the how, when and why of this that I would like to explore.

To Rudyard Kipling this concept was so important it inspired him to write a poem. Allow me to share with you the first few lines:

I have six trusty serving men,

They taught me all I know,

Their names are What, Why, When,

Where, How, and Who.

DUST TO DUST: *THE CYCLE OF LIFE*

To take reference from the oldest history book we have, the Bible says

> *In the sweat of thy face shalt thou eat bread, till thou return unto the ground; for out of it wast thou taken: for dust thou art, and unto dust shalt thou return.* Genesis 3:19

And again,

> *All go to one place; all are of the dust, and all turn to dust again.* Ecclesiastes 3:20

This is the verse the minister at the funeral is referring to when he says "ashes to ashes and dust to dust."

Science calls this process the Carbon Cycle, sometimes it is called the cycle of life. The Carbon Cycle is a description of how living matter is brought back to dust upon death of the organism.

The Carbon Cycle Illustrated

Cell damage causes microorganisms to change into:

What causes this process? Microorganisms. The soil of the earth is alive with microscopic organisms whose role it is to bring matter back to dust.

MICROORGANISMS IN THE DUST

An excellent example of the carbon cycle is the compost bin.

I have three compost bins.

Bin number one is the bin in which I am throwing the food scraps from the kitchen. I am also putting in the weeds from the garden, along with a good helping of cow manure.

Bin number two is the bin that is sitting and allowing the carbon cycle to work.

Bin number three is ready for the garden. The Carbon Cycle has brought all the vegetable matter back to dust and I can now put it in the garden.

What caused the vegetable matter to be brought back to dust?

Bacteria, fungi and yeast make up a large proportion of the microscopic life forms that live in the soil. They are responsible for breaking down dead matter and bringing it back to dust.

Bacteria, fungi and yeast make up a large proportion of the microscopic life forms that live in the soil.

They are also responsible for breaking down the minerals and metals in the soil, and converting them into an absorbable form that makes them available for the roots of the plants. It is these processes that cause compost to be an essential ingredient in the soil to produce healthy plants.

Fungi produce acid by-products that help them use nutrients in the minerals. This results in the return of essential nutrients and minerals like calcium, phosphate and potassium back into the soil where they can nourish plants and microbes.

Rocks are composed of minerals, the vast majority of which contain metals. They might be considered an inhospitable habitat for life to flourish, yet here fungi can thrive in the harshest of environments. These microscopic life forms can remain inactive or dormant for decades. But as soon as the environment provides a food source, they become active again.

There is a law of science that states, "Nothing is created and nothing is destroyed." These life forms cannot be destroyed, but they have the ability to change form, depending on the environment. Sometimes they may lay dormant for a long time—some for thousands of years—then become active when a good food source arrives.

Mosby's Medical Dictionary defines fungi as:

> A eukaryotic (contains a nucleus), thallus-forming organism that feeds by absorbing organic molecules from its surroundings. Fungi lack chlorophyll and are therefore not capable of photosynthesis. They may be saprophytes (eat dead organisms) or parasites (feed off living organisms). Unicellular fungi (yeasts) reproduce by budding; multicellular fungi (mould) reproduce by spore formation. Fungi may invade living organisms, including humans as well as non-living organic substances. Of the 100,000 identified species of fungi, 100 are common in humans and 10 are pathogenic (capable of causing disease).

The *Bantam Medical Dictionary* defines fungi as:

> Simple plants that lack the green pigment, chlorophyll. Fungi include yeasts, rusts, moulds and mushrooms. They live as either saprophytes or as parasites of plants and animals. Some species infect and cause diseases in man. The single-celled microscopic yeasts are a good source of vitamin B and many antibiotics are obtained from the moulds.

Classification of fungi has been a concern since the 17th century because they are neither animal nor plant, but contain some characteristics of both.

Fungi play a crucial role on planet Earth as:

- The clean-up team or garbage collectors. They accomplish this task by breaking down dead matter and bringing it back to dust. (The Carbon Cycle.)
- The producers of carbon dioxide in the soil for plant respiration.
- Agents that produce acids that convert metals and minerals in the soil to an absorbable form for the plants.

In other words, a fungal cell has a nucleus like an animal cell. In the yeast form, fungi are able to breathe without the use of oxygen (anaerobically) just like plants and yet they have no chlorophyll; fungi reproduce by spores and obtain nutrition from their environment (whether alive, dead or non-living organisms).

MICROORGANISMS IN PLANTS

Microbes are essential to the plant's existence and health. The plant moves 50 percent of its glucose to the roots each night and 60 percent of this is released to feed hoards of microorganisms surrounding the roots.

It is a classic example of the universal law "give and you shall receive". The plant is well rewarded for this gift. These microbes fix nitrogen from the atmosphere, recycle minerals from plant residues, remove toxins, stabilise locked up phosphorus, produce plant growth stimulants and protect the plant from pathogens.

The same microorganisms that are active in the growth and development of the plant also accomplish its breakdown. An apple grows by the action of these microorganisms. The same microorganisms ripen the apple. If not eaten, the microorganisms will also cause it to rot. The environment dictates the role, phase, function and form of each organism.

MICROORGANISMS IN THE EGG

Consider a mother hen sitting on ten eggs—all have the potential to hatch into a chicken. Imagine if I take one egg and shake it violently, then place it back under mother hen. In several weeks the sound of chirping reveals little life forms called chickens, emerging from the eggs. What caused the egg to develop into a chicken? It was the microorganisms contained in the white and yolk of the egg. We notice one egg has been kicked from the nest perhaps due to a bad smell emitting from it. What caused this smell? The cell damage caused by the shaking, required the microorganisms in that egg to change into bacteria, yeast, fungus and mould to accomplish their role in the Carbon Cycle and bring the damaged tissue back to dust.

MICROORGANISMS IN HUMANS

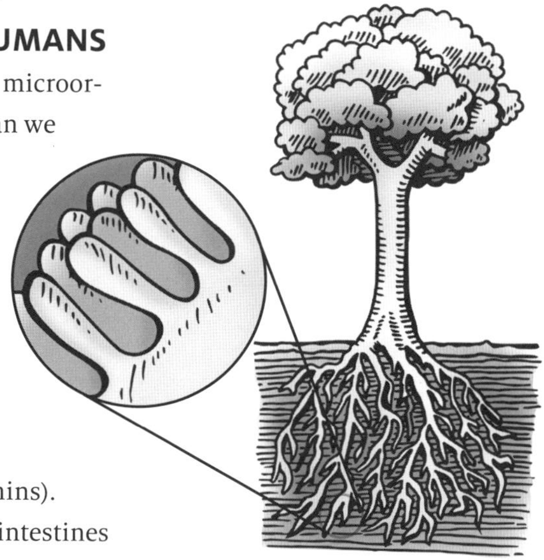

The human body contains more microorganisms than cells. (Does that mean we are more plant than animal?)

The largest concentration of the body's microorganisms is found in the gastrointestinal tract. Here they play a similar role as they do in the soil, they are breaking down some of the nutrients in our food into absorbable forms (specifically the B vitamins).

The tiny villi that line our small intestines can be likened to the roots of the plant. Just as the chlorophyll (the plants blood system) in the roots of the plants absorbs the nutrients in the soil that have been broken down by these microscopic life forms, so too does the blood supply in our villi absorb the nutrients that have been broken down in our gastrointestinal tract by microscopic life forms. Acidophilus and bifidus are the two permanent bacteria that live in the gastrointestinal tract. There are many other bacteria but they are transitory.

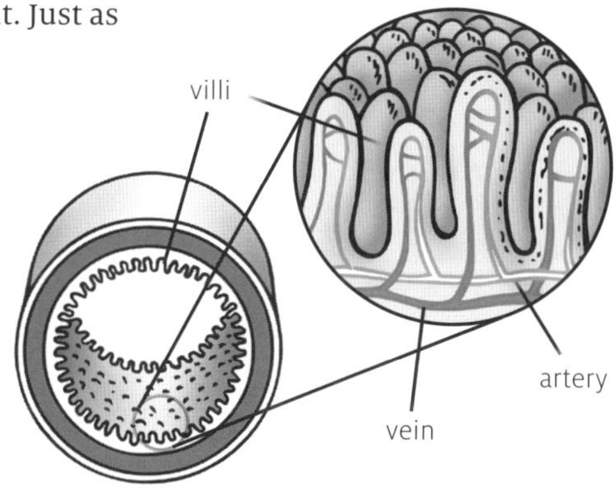

Bacteria, yeast and fungus are everywhere. These single-celled forms of life live on our skin, our hair, in our mouth, in our intestines and on the food we eat. Not only do they play a role in aiding the absorption of certain nutrients, they also protect us from harmful microbes.

Candida albicans is a yeast that lives in our gastrointestinal tract. This yeast plays an important role in the chemical balance in our intestines. Lactobacillus- acidophilus and bifidus bacterium are the bacteria that protect us from this yeast over colonising.

There are dozens of different species of candida. Approximately eight are known to cause disease in man. Broad spectrum antibiotic treatment kills off acidophilus and bifidus allowing candida to multiply at an aggressive rate. The overgrowth of these yeasts causes them to pass through the mucosal lining and leak into the blood stream. This is a common way this form of yeast can cause disease in humans.

Understanding the role of bacteria, fungus and yeast in nature gives us an indication of how these can affect humans. As we have already acknowledged, they have their two main roles: saprophytes and parasites.

Saprophytes feed off dead organisms. This includes any area in the human body that sustains damage from poisoning or trauma creating an environment conducive to fungal growth.

Parasites feed off living organisms. Fungi are able to live in the human body feeding off its tissues. They can enter in various ways—I will cover this later in the book.

So it is seen that some fungus feeds off dead organisms operating as nature's garbage disposal, while other parasitic fungus, feeds off live organisms.

These pathogenic fungi cause plant, animal and human diseases. Some of the simpler and more well known are athlete's foot (tinea), swimmer's ear, ringworm, dandruff, finger and toenail infections, rosacea and yeast infections.

Typically fungi sprout from a spore and grow as filaments termed hyphae. These hyphae extend at their tips and enable the fungus to grow continuously into fresh zones of nutrients and also to penetrate hard surfaces such as plant cell walls, insect cuticles, human skin and nails, and so on. This is why fungi are so important as plant pathogens and as decomposer organisms. Yeast transforms itself and grows hyphae very well at 37.5ºC (99.5ºF) which is body temperature. This explains why athlete's foot is a systemic condition. It has grown very deep into the tissues.

A LIVING ILLUSTRATION

Let us look at how the Carbon Cycle can function in a human body as an attempt to repair or heal cell damage.

Sick Steve is 35 years old and has smoked 15 to 20 cigarettes a day for 15 years. Cell damage is constantly happening in sick Steve's lungs. Tobacco, with its nicotine and approximately 4,000 other chemicals, does nasty things to every part of the body that it touches. Steve's microorganisms are evolving constantly into the "clean up brigade" (bacteria) in an attempt to keep his lungs working. Sick Steve is often coughing since this is how his lungs eliminate the waste from the clean up.

> *If* germs do cause disease, *if* Pasteur was right, Sick Steve and Healthy Harry should both have come down with the cold. But only Sick Steve becomes sick.

Sick Steve has a brother named Healthy Harry. Sick Steve thinks that Healthy Harry is a fitness fanatic. He exercises for an hour every day, drinks two to three liters of water every day and eats a lot of fresh fruit and vegetables, wholegrains, legumes, nuts and seeds. He does not drink alcohol, take drugs or even smoke cigarettes. Sick Steve thinks that Healthy Harry is dead boring.

One day their Cousin Colin visits. Colin has a bad cold. He coughs on both Sick Steve and Healthy Harry. The bacteria that are active in "spring cleaning" Cousin Colin are catapulted into Sick Steve. After a quick scout around, the bacteria discover a veritable banquet in Sick Steve's respiratory system. They even meet up with some relatives already feasting. As is their habit, they multiply rapidly. Coupled with the enzymes they release to digest their meal and the waste given off from the digestion of their meal, a toxic load is produced. This causes Sick Steve to rush to the doctor complaining of a terrible cold given to him by Cousin Colin. Now Sick Steve is really sick!

These same microorganisms that entered Sick Steve also entered Healthy Harry. But there was nothing to eat, very little waste to feed on and nothing in Healthy Harry's food program to feed on either. As the food supply was so poor, these microorganisms failed to thrive and were forced into dormancy.

If germs do cause disease, *if* Pasteur was right, Sick Steve and Healthy Harry should both have come down with the cold. But only Sick Steve becomes sick.

Meanwhile, in the doctor's office, Sick Steve describes the foul lumps that he is coughing up and how terrible he feels. He is all clogged up with mucus, his muscles ache and he feels like death warmed up. The doctor agrees. Sick Steve has caught a terrible cold from his cousin. The doctor prescribes an antibiotic to kill the unwelcome invader. Sick Steve begins his medication immediately, breathing a sigh of relief. To celebrate, he treats himself to his favourite meal of baked mushrooms on fresh yeast bread with blue vein cheese and a large steak. He washes this down with a few large glasses of beer, nibbling on a few peanuts as he drinks. To finish the meal he has a large bowl of ice cream covered in chocolate syrup.

Within six to eight hours, Sick Steve is experiencing relief from the symptoms of his cold. The bacteria that were having a party in his respiratory tract have suffered a lethal blow from the action of the antibiotics and the toxic waste they were producing has been reduced.

What is now happening in Sick Steve? Let us pull the curtain aside and have a look at the activity of these microscopic life forms in Sick Steve's body.

Unknowingly, Sick Steve has given the perfect food to the yeast and fungus now multiplying nicely in his body. For not only did the antibiotics kill off the bacteria in his lungs, but also the bacteria that forms the flora in his intestines. Now that they are reduced, the yeast that resides there (Candida albicans), begins to multiply. When yeast and fungus are introduced into the body in this way and allowed to multiply, they feed on cell damage and the yeast and sugar that are fed to it by the host (the human). They multiply quickly. The waste they give off is highly toxic to the body.

As already mentioned, several dozen candida species exist, and eight are known to cause disease in humans. The overgrowth of Candida albicans in the intestinal tract causes damage to the gut wall allowing subsequent passage through the mucosa lining of the gut into the bloodstream. This basically means the yeast can poke holes in the intestines allowing the yeast and partially digested food to enter the bloodstream. Because the white blood cells consider these to be enemies, this is one of the causes of many autoimmune diseases.

Let's see how Sick Steve is doing. His bad cold did die down but another problem developed. Sick Steve now has a bad case of jock itch around his scrotum, anal itch and tinea between his toes. He also notices that his tongue is heavily coated. These are all fungal outbreaks. Sick Steve returns to the doctor who gives him a course of nystatin. This antifungal medication causes the fungus to mutate and go deeper into the tissues.

In an attempt to alleviate the common cold, a far greater dilemma has been created, and poor old Steve is really sick!

In his ignorance, Sick Steve is caught up in a vicious cycle. His food and lifestyle habits are slowly killing him.

CAUSE AND EFFECT

Newton's third law of motion states that: "To every action there is an equal and opposite reaction" or, simply put, the law of cause and effect.

"This law never ceases to act as the perfect balancer. Nature's equaliser; setting into motion compensatory forces to remedy every imbalance," says David Phillips in his book *From Soil to Psyche.*

I NOW UNDERSTAND WHY ANTIBIOTICS ARE CALLED 'WONDER DRUGS', ANY TIME THE DOCTOR WONDERS WHAT A PATIENT HAS, THAT'S WHAT THEY GET.

ANTIBIOTICS—ARE THEY FRIEND OR FOE?

What are antibiotics, where did they come from, how do they affect the body, and what is the long-term effect of their use on the body?

In 1928, Alexander Fleming discovered that the spore from a mouldy orange on a fruit platter in the upstairs window had killed the bacteria he was growing in a flask in his downstairs laboratory. Alexander Fleming named the mould *penecillium,* and the mould waste, penecillic acid. The mould waste, or mycotoxin, is far more toxic than the mould itself. The mycotoxin is designed to kill off anything that would compete with its food source. This is a survival mechanism to ensure survival of the mould by protecting the source of food from any competition.

Antibiotics have saved millions of lives by killing off bacteria, thus eliminating them and the toxic waste they produce. This cannot be denied. The human body can cope with one or two courses of antibiotics in a lifetime. But there is a dangerous situation happening today with the overuse of antibiotics and the failure to question why the bacteria, yeast and fungus are so active in the body. One percent of doctors today are claiming that antibiotics are causing more problems than they have cured.

Remember anything that kills one organism (bacterium) in small doses has the ability to kill much larger organisms (humans) in large or repeated doses.

With the discovery of penicillium, hundreds of different mycotoxins were tested as possible antibiotics; 80 percent of them were deadly, too toxic to use. Antibiotics are antibacterial and antihuman substances. They not only kill off bacteria as in Sick Steve's lungs—which by the way were cleaning up his cell damage—they also kill the healthy bacteria living in the human gut; for example, bifidus bacterium and lactobacillus acidophilus. This now clears the way for yeast living also in the gut—Candida albicans—to multiply at an alarming rate.

To indicate how quickly yeast can multiply we have to look no further than yeast bread. It doubles in half an hour.

—CHAPTER TWO—

Historical Moments

What does the past tell us?

"The curse causeless shall not come."

—Proverbs 26:2

There are many great minds from the last two centuries whose quest for the true cause of disease has led them to the conclusion that fungus plays a major role in human diseases.

We will look at them later. But let us now view a sample of the thoughts of a few of these great names as we consider this theory.

An example of this theory in history:

Florence Nightingale (1820–1910). Florence led the nurses caring for thousands of soldiers during the Crimean War and helped save the British army from medical disaster. Conditions at the military hospital at the port in Scutari (modern-day Üsküdar in Istanbul) were so appalling that the death rate was up to 50 percent—higher than the battle front! When this report reached England, Florence was asked to take a team of nurses to see if they could help.

In November 1855, a team of nurses, under Florence's direction, began scrubbing and cleaning. The following month, a shipload of clean linen, bed clothes, bandages, scrubbing brushes and a cook arrived, courtesy of Florence's father. By April 1856, the death rate had fallen to 12 percent and within six months it had lowered still further to 2 percent.

This famous British nurse, who changed history by her radical treatment of disease using improved nutrition, hygiene and sanitation, wrote a book called *Notes on Nursing* in 1860. In her first paragraph Florence states:

> *Shall we begin by taking it as a general principle—that all disease, at some period, or other of its course, is more or less a reparative process, not necessarily accompanied by suffering: an effort of nature to remedy a process of poisoning or of decay, which has taken place weeks, months, sometimes years beforehand, unnoticed, the termination of the disease being then, while the antecedent process was going on determined?*

Here Florence Nightingale calls disease a process of repair. In other words, disease is actually our friend and the means by which our body repairs itself. If given the right conditions the body will repair, but if that process of repair is inhibited by such things as drugs, dehydration, malnutrition, or other neglect of health principles, then the very process designed to repair us may kill us. Notice that Florence states that disease is actually an effort of nature to remedy a process of poisoning or decay. In the poisoning process it is the microforms that clean up the mess.

What is decay? Surely it is another condition arising from poor lifestyle habits, again requiring the action of these small microforms.

Professor Antoine Bechamp (1816-1908) was a French professor who was famous for his many years of experiments on these microscopic life forms. In one experiment he took a dead cat and sealed it in an airtight container. Four months later he opened it and found dust and bones. What caused the breakdown? The microscopic life forms that were so vital to the life of the cat evolved into the clean-up brigade (bacteria) upon its death. Then followed the exterminators (yeast/fungus) and the undertakers (mould), successfully fulfilling their roles in the cycle of life by bringing matter back to dust. Bechamp took some of the dust and placed it under his microscope. It was alive with microscopic life forms. Once they had completed their role in the Carbon Cycle they then 'devolved' back into the form of microorganisms found in the dust.

A look at the now deceased cat's dust under the microscope revealed life —microorganisms.

THE CARBON CYCLE IN ACTION:

The cell damage in the cat (death) caused
the microorganisms to evolve into:

↓

Bacteria (Garbage collectors)

↓

Yeast/Fungus (Exterminators)

↓

Mould (Undertakers)

↓

DUST

As the environment changes, so does the role of
these players in the great cycle of life.

—CHAPTER THREE—

Familiarising with a Fungus Feast

Fungus is a living microorganism that is neither plant nor animal. Being a living organism, however, it must have food. It is estimated that there are 1.5 million different fungi, but their palate is similar. The more of its favourite food it can find, the more vigorous will be the fungus growth.

FUNGI'S FAVOURITE FEAST

Sugar in all its forms is fungi's favourite feast. The pure, crystallised acid that is extracted from the sugar cane or sugar beet plants is a particularly potent way to cause any fungus in the body to multiply quickly. Although fungus prefers the highly sweetened form of sugar extracted from the sugar cane, if this is denied, the fungus will accept honey, maple syrup and the sugar found in fruits; it is not fussy as to where the sugar comes from.

When the following foods are consumed, fungal growth is encouraged.

- All alcoholic beverages contain mycotoxins or yeasts.

- Yeast bread contains live yeast spore. While sourdough bread does contain small amounts of wild yeast, these do not pose a problem as they come in combination with lactobacillus, a "friendly" bacteria that can help break down food, absorb nutrients, and fight off diseases.
- Peanuts and cooked rice are both extremely susceptible to mould growth.
- Brewer's Yeast, and yeast extract spreads all contain yeast.
- Mushrooms are a fungus and need to be eliminated when endeavouring to eradicate fungus from the body.
- Mouldy food. Any food that has a trace of mould on it must not be eaten. This includes aged cheeses which are commonly infused with mould to create the cheeses' distinctive flavours (take a visit to a cheese factory and observe).

THE FUNGAL EVOLUTION IN THE HUMAN BODY

Many people are sick today because unhealthy lifestyle habits are causing cell damage in the body, requiring the body's own microorganisms to evolve into a clean-up brigade (bacteria) as part of the compensatory forces. If the bad habits continue, the bacteria can evolve into yeast and fungus, just as they do in the natural world.

Most foods today contain added sugar, which supplies these microforms with their favourite food allowing them to multiply unhindered. The waste from these microforms is toxic and can cause disease.

If mould or fungus enters the body in the spore form, it can only survive and flourish providing there is a good food supply.

THE FUNGAL INVASION IN THE HUMAN BODY

Another cause of sickness can come from an invasion of fungus and mould wastes, which can enter the human body in four ways:

Ingestion—eating mouldy food or taking antibiotics.

Inhalation—breathing in mould from compost or damp mouldy areas in buildings, carpet and even mattresses and pillows.

Via the Skin—mould spores can enter through the pores of the skin.

Sexual Transmission—fungus can travel via body fluids from one person to another.

If mould or fungus enters the body in the spore form, it can only survive and flourish providing there is a good food supply. In extreme cases some very virulent forms, when entering in large numbers, can cause death quite quickly.

DEFINING THE FUNGI PALLET IN THE HUMAN BODY

1. Waste

As exterminators, the role of fungus on planet Earth is to clear dead and decaying matter. Anywhere in the body where cell damage/death is occurring, these microforms—bacteria, fungi and yeast—will be.

2. Chemicals

Every year new chemicals are introduced. Some are found in herbicides, others in insecticides and pesticides. Residues of these are in all non-organically grown fruits, vegetables, nuts and grains. Meat, chicken and fish are commonly contaminated, as are dairy products and eggs.

Toxic chemicals are found in many household cleaning products as well as laundry detergents, soaps, shampoo, toothpaste, perfumes and makeup. When clothes made with nylon, acrylic and polyester are worn, these fibres release chemicals that the skin can absorb, especially when the person wearing them gets hot and begins to perspire.

These environmental poisons create free radicals that damage living tissue. In the cycle of life, these damaged tissues are a food supply for the opportunistic microorganisms—bacteria, yeast and fungi.

3. Synthetic Hormones

Synthetic hormones are contained in the contraceptive pill and hormone replacement therapy. Most synthetic hormone therapies contain oestrogen. Oestrogen's role in the body is that of a cell proliferator, causing massive cell growth. High levels of oestrogen cause yeast and fungus to multiply very quickly. Dr. John Lee, Dr. Sandra Cabot and Dr. Sherrill Sellman are among several authors who have written excellent books on how to balance your hormones naturally. Family Planning Clinics in most large towns provide information on natural birth control as an alternative to the pill. Perhaps not as convenient, but definitely not life threatening.

4. Heavy Metals

For the past fifty years, dentistry has been using metal amalgam fillings in teeth. These amalgam fillings can be 40–60 percent mercury. Over the years this mercury is absorbed and accumulates in the tissues of the body in the most toxic form, methyl mercury. Mercury is neurotoxic. There is no safe dose in humans. Fungus effectively breaks down heavy metals in the soil and so can also feed on heavy metals that accumulate in the tissues of the human body.

There are many excellent alternatives today to mercury fillings, which are just as strong yet not as toxic, with the added benefit of being cosmetically desirable.

—CHAPTER FOUR—

Fascinating Fungus

Mycology

The study of fungi

Mycology began with the discovery of aflatoxin in the early 1960s. Disease due to fungus, however, has been known from Bible times. The King James version of the Bible talks about leprosy of the skin, leprosy of the house and leprosy of the clothes. In modern translations leprosy of the house is called mildew. Leprosy in clothes is also interpreted as mildew, but leprosy of the skin is interpreted as infectious skin disease, though if following the former rules of translation, the latter should be interpreted as mildew of the skin.

It has been well documented that mycotoxins (fungal waste) cause disease in plants, animals and humans.

The total number of mycotoxins is not known but toxic metabolites (waste) of fungi potentially could number in the millions. Mycotoxins are produced by yeast/fungi and moulds. They are the 'urine and faeces', so to speak, which are produced as the fungi consume their food. The toxicity of these mycotoxins is designed to kill off anything that would compete with the fungi food source. Certain mycotoxins function as potential virulence factors in producing disease in plants, animals and humans.

According to the *American Council of Agricultural Science and Technology* (CAST), it is not possible to estimate precisely the economic cost of mycotoxins. Their rough estimate of food and stock feed losses came up with the figure of $932 million per year for the US alone. This figure was for 2003 and would quite possibly be higher now.

With approximately 84% of the UK population living in urban areas,[1] food must be grown in large amounts and thus stored in large amounts. This is one of the reasons why grains infected with moulds/fungi are now a problem. Corn, wheat and peanuts are the most commonly affected. Silos where these grains are stored commonly sustain moisture contact thus giving the perfect environment for mould/fungal growth.

MOST COMMONLY FOUND MYCOTOXINS IN FOODS

Aspergillus, Penicillium, Fusarium are three of the most potentially toxic fungal species found infecting grains.

Aflatoxin, Ochratoxin, Trichothecenes, Zearalenone, Fumonisin, Citreoviridum, Penicillic acid and Gliotoxin are some of the disease-causing mycotoxins that these fungi produce.

Aflatoxin. Believed to be the most carcinogenic substance ever tested. Aflatoxicosis is well documented, and has many times linked aflatoxin to hepatocellular carcinoma (liver cancer).

Other studies also link aflatoxin with cancer in the gastrointestinal tract and liver. These particular studies were in Africa, the Philippines, China and in India, where the mortality reached 25 percent. Kwashiorkor and Reye's syndrome have been associated with aflatoxin in food.[2]

Aflatoxins were detected in liver tissue of 36 children with Kwashiorkor. In 1994, research in Shanghai demonstrated a specific biomarker for aflatoxin is related to human liver cancer, and that hepatitis B virus and aflatoxin B interact as risk factors for liver cancer.[3]

Aflatoxin B1 is a known contaminant in cured tobacco, thus it is highly likely to be in the smoke.

Aflatoxin B1 is known to cause mutations in the tumour suppressor gene.

Aflatoxin is commonly found in corn and peanuts.

Ochratoxins. A mycotoxin produced primarily by the moulds Aspergillus or Penicillium that occurs on several commodities prevalent in human diets; for example, cereal grains and peanuts. It's known for its effect primarily on the kidneys but can also affect the liver. A major renal disease in swine occurs in some European countries, especially Denmark, and is associated with consumption of ocharatoxin contaminated barley.[4]

In 1956, the first clinical description of a human kidney disease, known as Balkan Endemic Nephropathy with unknown cause, was published. Ochratoxin has been strongly linked to this disease, especially since this mycotoxin has been found in the food of patients from the Balkan countries.

Guinea pigs and rabbits experimentally exposed to air passed through a layer of the ochratoxin-contaminated wheat experienced renal failure.

Intestinal microflora can convert Ochratoxin A into Ochratoxin alpha, a non-toxic metabolite that can be measured in the urine and faeces.

OF COURSE I'LL NEED TO RUN SOME TESTS; BUT OFFHAND I'D SAY IT'S SOME SORT OF FUNGUS INFECTION.

Trichothecenes. This mycotoxin is a potent protein inhibitor, which is the basic mechanism of their toxicity. In Russia in 1944, a disease occurred known as Alimentary Toxic Aleukia, and was characterised by total recrotic angina. Mortality rates reached 80 percent. Patients experienced vomiting, diarrhoea, abdominal pain and burning in the upper gastrointestinal tract. This would occur shortly after eating contaminated food. It was caused by consuming over-wintered cereal grains or their products. The Fusarium organism was isolated from the grains after more than 20 years of storage. Fusarium is capable of producing the mycotoxin Trichothecenes—T2 toxin. These symptoms can be produced in cats when given purified T2 toxin orally.[5]

Zearalenone. In Puerto Rico in 1985, premature puberty occurred in seven- and eight-year-old children in epidemic proportions. Researchers examined local food and found high concentrations of the mycotoxin Zearalenone, which is an Estradiol equivalent in some of the meat. Zeoralanol is a processed anabolic product made from Zearalenone and approved for use as an anabolic agent in cattle and sheep in Puerto Rico. It appears that exposure could have been from mothers who ingested contaminated food during pregnancy.

Hsieh, in 1989, suggested that Zearalenone was possibly involved in human cervical cancer and premature puberty. Zearalenone has also been found in high concentrations in cereal foods (grains).

Fumonisin. An association between the consumption of mouldy corn and high human oesophageal cancer rates found in parts of Southern Africa[6] and the Linxian area of China[7] has been known for some time.

Oesophageal cancer rates and the consumption of corn products, which likely contain Fumonisins,[8] have simultaneously increased in northern Italy in recent years.

Various Fusarium species are common in corn worldwide, but it is the consumption of food prepared from 'home grown' contaminated corn that has been correlated with oesophageal dysplasia (pre-cancerous), and also oesophageal cancer in southern Africa and China.[9]

Citreoviridum. Acute cardiac beri beri is a disease that occurred for centuries, including the early twentieth century in Japan and other Asian countries. It was characterised by rapid pulse, palpitations, vomiting and low blood pressure, and led to respiratory failure and death (Veno 1974). A fungus was isolated and identified as Citreoviridum.[10] The Rice Act of 1921 passed by the Japanese government decreased the availability of mouldy rice in the markets and resulted in a rapid decline of the disease.[11]

Gliotoxin. This immunosuppressive mycotoxin first attracted the interest of investigators searching for new antibiotics. However, its toxicity precluded clinical use as an antibiotic. (Many proposed fungal antibiotics were never marketed because their toxicity precluded their clinical use). Interest in Gliotoxin was revived when it was discovered to be produced by Aspergillus fumigatus and other such fungi as Candida Albicans, and that it had unusual immunosuppressive activities. This toxin has been found in vaginal secretions of women with Candida Vaginitis. The involvement of Gliotoxin in the pathogenesis of Aspergillosis and Candidiasis could be important because the immunosuppressive nature of this toxin could exacerbate the infection and possibly be a virulence factor. Immune-suppression is a major effect of mycotoxins.[11]

Chapter Four References

1 Aaron O'Neill (2023), Urbanisation in the United Kingdom 2021. *Statista*, accessed December 202 <https://www.statista.com/statistics/270369/urbanization-in-the-united-kingdom/>

2 Council for Agricultural Science and Technology (2003) *Mycotoxins: Risks in Plant, Animal and Human Systems*, Task Force Report No 139, January 2003, page 50.

3 ibid.

4 CAST, op cit, page 51.

5 ibid, page 52.

6 Marasas, WFO, Jaskiewicz, K, Venter, FS, and Van Schalkwyk, DJ (1988). Fusarium moniliforme contamination of maize in oesophogeal cancer areas in Transkei. *South African Medical Journal*, Vol 74, pages 110–114.

7 Yang, CS, (1980) Research on esophageal cancer in China: a review. *Cancer Research Journal*, Vol 40, pages 2633–2644.

8 Dōko, MB and Visconti, A (1994), Occurrence of fumonisins B1 and B2 in corn and corn-based human foodstuffs in Italy. *Food Additives and Contaminants*, Vol 11 No 4, pages 433-439.

9 CAST, op cit, page 54.

10 Miyake and Igaku 1943, cited in *Ueno* 1974.

11 CAST, op cit, page 53.

12 ibid, page 56.

—CHAPTER FIVE—

Presenting the Evidence History of Fungus

The role fungus plays in human disease

"There is nothing new under the sun."
—ECCLESIASTES 1:9

As has been established, fungi are everywhere and can cause disease in humans. The first known documented description of fungus is in the Bible. As previously mentioned the older versions call it leprosy. The newer versions call it mildew. The Bible talks about mildew in the clothes, in the house and on the skin. Notice the description, "He (the authorities) is to examine the mildew on the walls of the house and if it has greenish or reddish depressions" (Leviticus 14:37)—a vivid description of fungus!

The account goes on to explain how the stones of the house with the mildew had to be thrown outside the city. The house then had to be scraped and the dust discarded. Next, other stones were to be put in the place of the discarded stones and plastered in. If the mildew returned after this process then the authorities would declare it 'unclean', and the house had to be destroyed.

The remnants were to be taken out of the city to an 'unclean' place—this may seem like an overreaction to us. To take such action reveals that mildew was considered dangerous and deadly! The Hebrew word for leprosy is the same word used for leprosy of the skin, house and clothes. In a modern translation of the Bible, the translators have used the word mildew in place of leprosy when discussing houses and clothes. But instead of calling the condition 'mildew of the skin', when discussing skin, they have called it 'infectious skin disease'. Science today reveals the fungal link with skin diseases.

Today more and more doctors and scientists are discovering the fungal link with disease. But it is not new to today's biologists and mycologists.

Today more and more doctors and scientists are discovering the fungal link with disease. But it is not new to today's biologists and mycologists.

In the book *The Germ that Causes Cancer,* Doug Kaufman explores the role of fungus in human disease.

In one section of this fascinating book, Kaufman discusses the work of Dr. Milton White, a scientist who has published medical articles for more than 50 years. His search for the cause of cancer led him to see the relationship between fungus and disease. Kaufman explains it well:

> *Dr.. White writes that the spores from the Asomycete fungi are involved in cancer's cause. Asomycete fungi are the class of fungi whose spores require a container in which to lie dormant. The container is actually a very durable sac. It cannot be destroyed using strong caustics, by boiling, or by alternate freezing and thawing of the sac.*
>
> *Upon entry into a human host, this spore is deprived of atmospheric oxygen and exposed to a temperature of 98.6 degrees F (or 36 degrees C),—human body temperature. In this new environment, the spore thrives even in the absence of oxygen as it begins to shed its durable sac. Without its hard covering, the spore, referred to as a 'deficient form' (ie. deficient of its environmental enclosure), is now free to invade human cells as a liberated*

> *fungal spore. Spore reproduction begins inside the human cell.*[1]
> *Systemic infection can be caused by ascomycete candida in its spore form. The adult form of this fungus is not capable of causing serious disease but may play a role in inflammation. The ascomycete fungi are a large class of true fungi, the sac fungi, which includes true yeasts, blue moulds and penicillium.*
> *Once inside the body, the fungal spores shed their protective cell walls in order to use human cells as sacs. These 'egg' spores can lay dormant in nature or inside the human body for years. There are a number of 'dormancy breakers' that can cause spore reproduction. The availability of the fungis' favourite food—sugar—and a high carbohydrate diet or antibiotics or depressed immune system or certain hormones. These dormancy breakers can be the biggest risk factors in the invasion of humans' fungi.*[2]

The fungal spores in their cell wall and deficient forms inside the human cell are able to incorporate their DNA with the human DNA to create a hybrid or mutated cell. The cell now changes from aerobic (in the presence of oxygen) to anaerobic (the absence of oxygen) respiration.

This anaerobic respiration gives off lactic acid, which in turn lowers the pH of the body. Fungus and disease thrive in an acid pH.

In her book, *Cell Wall Deficient Forms,* Ida Mattman further explains how the fungi can merge into a human cell:

> *Chemical analyses show that the walls of these organisms have a high lipid (fat) content. This explains why they wash from slides and why they melt to artefacts when the slide is heat-fixed. Which is why the cover slip is needed on the slide.*
> *These organisms are tiny and they slip into erythrocytes (red blood cells), thanks to pinocytosis (the ability of certain substances to be able to merge into the cell). Within the red blood cell they are protected from phagocytosis (destruction) by immune cells (white blood cells) and have transportation to all areas of the body.*[3]

As the fungal cell is now merged with the human cell, it escapes destruction by the white blood cell because the white blood cell now sees it as a human cell.

PLEOMORPHISM *(many forms)*

Pleomorphism describes the changing role of microbes in the human body. Pleomorphism is the Carbon Cycle in action. Medicine today is based on Louis Pasteur's theory of monomorphism, which states that bacteria is only ever bacteria, or fungus is only ever fungus. The following scientists and doctors have proven otherwise.

Professor Gunther Enderlein (1872-1968) called the tiny biological unit of life a 'protit'. It has since been named a microorganism. Enderlein observed when looking at live blood under a microscope that 'protits' remained small in response to a healthy condition as they built and worked within the body. But when these life units encountered a disturbed inner condition they enlarged and **change into more complex forms** including bacteria and fungus. This is called pleomorphism: relating to the ability of these small life units to change roles.

Antoine Bechamp (1816-1908) was a Master of Pharmacy, Doctor of Science, Doctor of Medicine, Professor of Medical Chemistry and Pharmacy, Fellow and Professor of Physics and Toxicology, Professor of Biological Chemistry and a Dean of Faculty of Medicine.

Bechamp named the microscopic forms of life that he viewed through the microscope 'microzymas' or small ferments, describing the microscopic life form's digestion as fermentation. For example, bacteria decompose dead leaves and rocks into dust. Bechamp stated, "Microzymas are at the beginning and end of all organisations".

He referred to 'microzymas' as the builders and destroyers of cells. "In the state of health the 'microzymas' act harmoniously and our life is in every sense of the word a regular fermentation." Whenever there is cell damage these 'microzymas' change their function and **turn into forms capable of more vigorous fermentative breakdown.** This led Bechamp to conclude: "Diseases are born of us and in us."

Claude Bernard (1813-1878) was a French physiologist. Bernard called the internal environment of the body 'The Terrain'. He maintained that the condition of 'The Terrain' was the most important in disease conditions, much more so than the microorganism, as the microorganism **changed its role** depending on the condition of 'The Terrain' (the body).

Royal Raymond Rife (1888-1971) built a microscope with 31,000 diameters revolution which was capable of detail and clarity surpassing any other microscope of its day, or even for that matter, our day. Weighing 200 pounds (90 kilograms), standing 2 feet (60 centimeters) high and containing 5,682 parts, it was an unsung wonder of the world. It used prismatically dispersed natural light. Royal Rife's work demonstrated beyond a shadow of a doubt that microscopic life forms are pleomorphic. A major upshot of his work was his ability through several pleomorphic stages, to **transform a virus he found in cancer tissues into a fungus**, plant the fungus into an asparagus-based medium, and produce bacillus E coli, the type of microform found in the human intestine. He repeated this hundreds of times.

The Mayo Clinic's Dr. Edward Rosenon wrote as early as 1914 in the *Journal of Infectious Diseases* that "It would seem that focal (mouth) infections are no longer looked upon merely as a place of entrance of bacteria but as a place where conditions are favourable for them to acquire the properties that give them **a wide range of affinities for various structures.**"

Dr. Virginia Livingston, in 1947, discovered a pleomorphic organism in all cancers she studied. She found it could be both helpful and unhelpful to the body, and that it is "dormant until activated by the need to repair damaged cells". In 1953 with two other women doctors, **Dr. Diller** and **Dr. Jackson**, they presented an exhibit at a meeting of the American Medical Association with visual footage of **pleomorphic changes**. They showed the link between these microbes and cancer.

In 1974, **Ida H. Mattman** of the department of Biology Wayne State University published *Cell Wall Deficient Forms*. Though pleomorphism was a proven phenomenon, the orthodox school continued to ignore it. Mattman writes:

> *Current bacteriology holds the belief that each species of bacteria has only a certain simple form. . . in contrast, this writer, using carefully prepared*

pure cultures found that bacteria ***pass through stages with markedly different morphology.*** *Pleomorphic forms are the first growth in culture. Bacterial life is subject to a* ***series of diverse morphological stages,*** *only one of which is the classical rod, coccus, spirillum or spirochete. Granular, mycelial, and large body stages are all capable of reverting to the parent forms . . . the shape the variants adopt is largely determined by the presence and concentration of certain amino acids, carbohydrates, ions and gases in the environment."*[4]

Time lapse photography shows that many agents and conditions cause a bacterium to alter its morphology, exchanging a rigid format for a pleomorphic outline.

Florence Seibert, Professor Emeritus of the Biochemistry University of Pennsylvania, wrote the book on this subject *Pebbles on the Hill of a Scientist* in 1968. "We were able to isolate bacteria from every piece of tumour and every acute leukemia blood specimen we had." This was published in the *Annuls of the New York Academy of Sciences*: "One of the most interesting properties of these bacteria is their great pleomorphism. For example, they readily **change their shape** from round cocci, to elongate rods and even to long thread like filaments depending on what medium they grow on and how long they grow."

In a paper presented to the New York Academy of Sciences in 1969, **Dr. Virginia Livingston** and **Dr. Elenor Alexander Jackson** declared that a single cancer microorganism exists. They said that the reason an army of cancer researchers couldn't find it was that it **changed form**.
"The organism has remained an unclassified mystery, due in part to its **pleomorphism** and its stimulation of other microorganisms. Phases may resemble viruses, micrococci, diphtheroids, bacilli and fungi."

In 1980, French bacteriologists **Sorin Sonea** and **Maurice Parisset** published their book *A New Bacteriology*. The central theme of their book was that bacterial pleomorphism was now a scientific fact. They stated that, "different types of bacteria were only **different manifestations** of a unified bacterial world".

In 2001, **Dr. Robert Young** explained in his book *Sick and Tired* that he had made similar observations and had identified this pleomorphic cycle. He states that these microforms in live cells became bacteria, then yeast and fungus, and then became mould. The acids produced by these life forms are poisons and can poison the human body. The book contains photographs of slides taken of the microorganisms changing form.

These scientists are all describing a process well known on planet Earth as the Carbon Cycle. The Bible describes it in Genesis 3:19: "We came from dust and we return to dust."

The Carbon Cycle is demonstrated on the rainforest floor and in the compost bin. It is the microscopic life forms that cause this Carbon Cycle to happen.

The same microorganisms that cause an apple to grow also cause it to ripen, and also cause it to rot, bringing it back to dust. If the apple is damaged the Carbon Cycle can kick in earlier. The environment dictates the activity or role of these life forms. The final breakdown is accomplished by yeast, fungus and mould. They can be called the undertakers. This is their role on planet Earth.

A basic law of science states: "Nothing is created and nothing is destroyed". It changes form. This is pleomorphism.

If not for the important role of bacteria, fungus, yeast and mould, this planet would be covered in rubbish.

The medical textbook, *Principles and Practice of Clinical Mycology,* written by C.C. Kibbler in 1996, shows in detail the fungal link in every human disease.

Note the chapter titles:

The Fungal Kingdom: Essentials of Mycology
Pathogenesis of Fungal Diseases
Epidemiology of Fungal Diseases
Diagnosis of Fungal Diseases
Antifungal Therapy
Fungal Disease of Bone and Joint
Fungal Diseases of the Cardiovascular System
Fungal Meningitis
Mycoses Causing Mass Legions of the Central Nervous System
Fungal Disease in Dermatology

Fungal Infections of the Ear, Nose and Throat
Fungemia and Disseminated Fungal Infection
Fungal Infection of the Gastro-Intestinal Tract
Fungal Diseases in Genitourmary Medicine
Fungal Infections of the Kidney and those associated with Renal Failure, Dialysis and Renal Transplantation
Fungal Diseases in Ophthalmology
Fungal Infections of the Respiratory Tract

In Chapter 2, Kibbler states: "The escalating incidence of fungal infections is linked in part to the widespread use of broad-spectrum antibiotics and the advent of increasing numbers of patients with cancer and other underlying diseases receiving intensive immunosuppressant regimens."

I have included the following chart (from Kibbler's book) which gives a short and concise summary of common human fungal pathogens and the diseases they can cause.

Chapter Five References

1 Kaufman, D, (2002), *The Germ that Causes Cancer*, Mediatrition, page 124.
2 ibid, page 139.
3 Mattman, I, (2000, first published September 1974), *Cell Wall Deficient Forms*, Third Edition, CRC Press. page 10.
4 ibid, page 32.

Common human fungal pathogens and their diseases

Fungus genus or group	Pathogenic Species	Distinguishing Characteristics	Common type(s) of disease caused	Comments
Apsergillus	Many, of which A. flavus, A. fumigatus, A. niger and A terreus are the most important human pathogens	Ascomycetes. Conidia are produced in chains from phialides borne on characteristic swollen conidiophores	Bronchopulmonary allergy, otomycosis, pulmonary fungus balls, keratomycosis, localised pulmonary and disseminated invasive infections in immunocompromised hosts	
Blastomyces	B. dermatitides	Dimorphic ascomycete: develops in a budding yeast form in infected tissues, hyphal form with smooth, round conidia on stalks in cultures at temperatures below 30°C (86°F).	Blastomycosis: pulmonary lesions with frequent dissemination to skin. Other sites of infection known	Perfect stage is Ajellomyces dermatitides
Candida	Many, of which C. albicans, C. glabrata, C. guilliermondii, C. krusei, C. lusitaniea, C. parapsilosis and C. tropicalis are the most commonly encountered pathogenic species	Imperfect yeast genus with ascomycetous affinities. C. albicans can form true hyphae and chlamydospores under appropriate culture conditions. Species distinguished on basis of physiological properties as well as morphology	Mucosal and cutaneous lesions in normal hosts, extensive superficial and/or disseminated infections in immunosuppressed hosts	

Fungus genus or group	Pathogenic Species	Distinguishing Characteristics	Common type(s) of disease caused	Comments
Coccidioides	C. immitis	Dimorphic hyphomycete with ascomycetous affinities: develops as endosporulating spherules in infected tissues and as a mould with alternating arthroconidiea in the soil	Coccidioidomycosis: primary pulmonary infection that can disseminate to affect mainly skin, bone and central nervous system	
Cryptococcus	C. neoformans	Yeast with capsules: a basidiomycete that forms hyphae when strains are mated	Cryptococcosis: primary pulmonary infection that can disseminate to cause meningitis; skin involvement seen in some patients	Perfect stage is Filobasidiella neoformans
Dermatophytes	Many, of which Epidermophyton floccosum, Microsporum audouinii, M. canis, trichophyton mentagrophytes, T. rubrum, T. schoenleinii and T. tonsurans are the most commonly encountered	Ascomycetes that can form both macroconidia and microconidia in the imperfect forms that are isolated from clinical material	Dermatophytosis (tinea capitis, corporis, cruris, pedis etc.) with lesions in skin, hair and nail of immunologically intact hosts	Perfect stages are classified in the genus Arthroderma

Fungus genus or group	Pathogenic Species	Distinguishing Characteristics	Common type(s) of disease caused	Comments
Eumycetomoa agents	Many, of which Pseudallescheria boydii, Madurella grisea, M. mycetomatis and various Acremonium spp. are the most common	Moulds, mostly fungi imperfect, with a wide range of specific morphological characters	Mycetoma; localised, indolent, deforming tumour with draining sinuses and 'grains' or 'granules' of the causative agent in the infected tissues: arises from traumatic implantation	'Eumycetoma' specifically implies a fungal cause: 'mycetoma' may also be caused by filamentous bacteria
Histoplasma	H. capsulatum var. capsulatum, H. capsulatum var. duboisii	Dimorphic ascomycete that develops as budding yeasts in infected tissues and as hyphal mould in soil	Histoplasmosis; primary pulmonary infection that can disseminate to involve multiple deep organs	Perfect stage is Ajellomyces capsulatus
Loboa	L.loboi	Unclassified-—cannot be grown in laboratory culture	Lobomycosis; subcutaneous infection	
Malassezia	M. furfur	Dimorphic yeast requiring lipides as essential nutrients: spherical yeast forms and short, branched hypahe in infected tissues, spherical and ovoid yeast forms predominate in culture	Pityriasis vericolor, an epidermal infection: probably also involved in the aetiology of seborrhoeic dermatits and dandruff	The genus name Pityrosporum is well known but no longer a valid alternative to Malassezia M. pachydermatis causes otitis externa in dogs

Fungus genus or group	Pathogenic Species	Distinguishing Characteristics	Common type(s) of disease caused	Comments
Paracoccidiodes	P.brasiliensis	Dimorphic fungus that develops as yeasts with multiple buds in invaded tissues and as hyphal forms at temperatures lower than 37°C (98.6°F).	Paracoccidioidomycosis; mucocutaneous infections or pulmonary infections with tendency to disseminate to other deep organs and skin	
Phaeohyphomycosis agents	Many genera and species of dematiaceous (dark-coloured) moulds		Phaeohyphomycosis; lesions commonly involve subcutaneous, central nervous system or respiratory tract sites	
Piedraia	P.hortae	Dematiaceous mould; an ascomycete that forms abundant asci and swollen intercalary cells	Black piedra: a hair shaft infection	
Pneumocystis	P. carinii	Organism phenotypically resembles a protozoan but has been shown to have affinities with fungi at the level of RNA base sequences	Pneumocystis carinii pneumonia	
Pseudallescheria	P.boydii (Scedosporium apiospermum)	Ascomycete with ascospores produced within a cleistothecium	Multiple disease types (see also 'eumycetoma')	P. boydii is the perfect stage of S. apiospermum

Fungus genus or group	Pathogenic Species	Distinguishing Characteristics	Common type(s) of disease caused	Comments
Rhinosporidium	R. seeberi	Exists as sporangia (forming endospores) within infected tissues. Cannot be grown in laboratory	Rhinosporidiosis; polynoid masses affecting nose, nasopharynx and conjunctiva	
Sporothrix	S. schenckii	Dimorphic hyphomycete that develops in a budding yeast form in infected tissues and as a conidial mould below 37ºC (98.6ºF)	Sporotrichosis; commonly a lymphcutaneous infection arising from traumatic implantation, sometimes a pulmonary infection after inhalation	
Subcutaneous zygomycosis agents	Basidiobolus ranarum, Conidiobolus spp.	Zygomycetous fungi than can also produce conidia	Subcutaneous zygomycosis (entomophthoromycosis)	
Trichosporon	T. beigelii	Yeast-like fungus that forms abundant arthroconidia and blastoconidea. Probably a basidiomycete	White piedra: a hair shaft infection. May cause disseminated infection in immunosuppressed hosts	
Zyomycosis agents	Many, including Mucor spp., Rhizopus spp., Absidia spp. and many others	Zygomycetes differentiated according to structures of sporangia	Zygomycosis; respiratory tract infections with tendency to invade further locally or disseminate in some immununo-compromised hosts	

—CHAPTER SIX—

The Link Between Fungus and Cancer

As we have discussed, over the last century and before, many researchers have proven the fungal link in disease. Let us now look at some compelling evidence linking fungus with cancer over the last few decades.

Professor A.V Constantine, former head of the World Health Organization, Department of Mycology, has written several books in the *Fungal Bionic Series* showing the relationship between fungus and disease, including cancer. These books provide documentary evidence that fungi and their biological metabolites, the mycotoxins, are silent and relentless attackers of human health in that they cause the major 'degenerative' and 'cancerous' diseases that plague mankind. Constantine backs his theory with more than 20 years of research; his books were published in the late 1990s.

Doug Kaufmann has written a series of books also showing the relationship between fungus and disease. Three of his books *Fungal Link One, Two* and *Three* show the link with various diseases. But his most remarkable book called *The Germ That Causes Cancer* goes into the history of medicine in the

19th, 20th and beginning of the 21st century showing the alarming fact that the link between fungus and cancer has been known for over a hundred years. These books were published in the 1990s.

In 2007, **Dr. Tullio Simoncini** published a book called *Cancer is a Fungus: A revolution in the therapy of tumours*. Dr. Simoncini is a medical doctor and surgeon based in Rome who specialises in Oncology, Diabetology and Metabolic disorders. He is also a Doctor of Philosophy. After quoting much research to prove his theory, Simoncini states in his book: "Candida is truly the cancer and it must be fought from this standpoint in all its pathogenic variants." He has had quite phenomenal results by treating cancer with a very simple treatment that has been used to treat fungus in agriculture for many years—sodium bicarbonate.

Sodium bicarbonate is safe, extremely inexpensive, it can be bought in a supermarket for a few dollars and yet, it is a deadly killer to cancer cells for it hits them with a shock wave of alkalinity. This alkalinity allows a rush of oxygen into the cancer cell. Cancer cannot survive in the presence of high levels of oxygen. By making the terrain where the fungus is living completely inorganic, sodium bicarbonate eliminates the slightest organic material that fungus uses for nourishment. Sodium bicarbonate is currently used to treat oral candidiasis in children and appears to be such a simple and handy weapon in uprooting, inhibiting and even reversing any malignant growth wherever it is applied.

Simoncini uses a local application of sodium bicarbonate in solution where possible, but resorts to inserting catheters for areas that cannot be reached with local applications. He states that almost all organs can be treated with this therapy. He has found this to be a very powerful weapon against fungi in these areas, stating that its effectiveness is painless leaving no after effects with very low risks:

> *We have seen that fungi are able to quickly mutate their genetic structure. That means that after an initial phase of sensitivity to fungicides, in a short time they are able to codify them and to metabolise them without been damaged by them—rather paradoxically, they extract a benefit from their high toxicity on the organism.*[2]

In other words, many antifungal therapies may be effective at first but consistently lose their effectiveness with time.

Sodium bicarbonate instead, as it is extremely diffusible and without that structural complexity that fungi can easily codify, retains its ability to penetrate the masses for a long time. This is also and especially due to the speed at which it disintegrates them, which makes it impossible for the fungi to adapt so that it cannot defend itself.

Along with the sodium bicarbonate treatment, Simoncini stresses the importance of assessing the emotional health of the patient along with proper hydration and diet.[3]

Dr. T. Colin Campbell's book *The China Study* (2006) is being cited as one of the most important books on nutrition ever written. In the first few chapters of the book, Campbell talks about his early career, which was spent working with two of the most toxic chemicals ever discovered—Dioxin and Aflatoxin. He was asked to investigate the unusually high prevalence of liver cancer in Filipino children. This was linked to the high consumption of aflatoxin, a mould toxin found in peanuts and corn. In his research, the peanut butter the children consumed was found to have far higher levels of aflatoxin than standard peanuts. What startled Campbell was the high death rate amongst the wealthy children. He found that the wealthier Filipino families ate high amounts of meat and dairy products, compared to the poorer children who were on a traditional Chinese diet of mainly vegetables, rice, some soy and a little fish.

Around this time, a research paper from India surfaced in the *American Medical Association Journal.* The paper described an experiment observing the link between liver cancer and protein consumption in two groups of laboratory rats. One group was given aflatoxin and then fed a diet containing 20 percent animal protein. The second was given the same level of aflatoxin and then fed a diet containing just 5 percent animal protein. Every single rat fed 20 percent animal protein developed liver cancer or its precursor lesions, but not a single rat fed a 5 percent protein diet got liver cancer or its precursor lesions. This was not a trivial difference: it was a 100 percent versus 0 percent. Rarely in research do you get these results.[4]

As these results confirmed what Campbell was finding, he applied for funding and spent the next few decades researching this himself. Campbell and his team organised a very large study of several hundred rats. Rats generally live two years. The study was a hundred weeks in length. All animals that were administered aflatoxin and were fed 20 percent levels of casein (animal protein) were dead or near death from liver tumors at 100 weeks. All animals administered the same level of aflatoxin but fed the low 5 percent protein diet were alive, active and thriving with sleek hair coats at 100 weeks. This was a virtual 100 to 0 score. A result rarely seen in research and almost identical to the original research in India.[5, 6]

In his experiments, Campbell was surprised to find that plant protein did not promote cancer growth, even at a 20 percent level. When the rats were given 20 percent plant protein, the results were similar to a 5 percent animal protein response. In other words, the cancer protective effect given by 5 percent animal protein was also given with 20 percent plant protein.

Campbell discovered that low-protein diets or their equivalents (plant protein), reduce tumors by the following mechanisms:

- Less aflatoxin entered the cell
- Cells multiplied more slowly
- Multiple changes occurred within the enzyme complex to reduce its activity
- The quantity of critical components of the relevant enzymes was reduced
- Less aflatoxin-DNA adducts were formed.

So the question arrises, "what is 'enough' protein?" The recommend daily protein amount is 10% of your total daily calories. In comparison, the average American consumes around 16% of their daily calories in the form of protein[7] —this is among the highest worldwide.

Overloading your diet with protein can mess up your macronutrient balance. Eating high amounts of protein is usually achieved by eating lots of meat and dairy products. However substituting animal protein, especially from processed red meat, with plant protein is associated with lower mortality, suggesting the importance of protein source. As the research confirms, this amount of protein is not a problem if it comes from plants.[8]

The October 2007 Australian edition of *Time* presented a very interesting article on breast cancer. In the section 'Western Ways, Western Woes' it stated that, "If the spread of US and European lifestyles is indeed contributing to the breast cancer boom, the first and worse of all those new habits is almost surely diet. In a study released in July, scientists traced the eating habits of 3000 Chinese women ranging in age from 25-64. Half of the group ate a 'meat-sweet' diet of Western cuisine, rich in red meat, shrimp, fish, candy, pudding, bread and milk. The others stuck to more traditional Asian fare of vegetables, sprouts, beans, tofu, fish and soy milk. Post-menopausal women in the 'meat-sweet' group showed a 60 percent greater risk of developing the most common kind of breast cancer."

Dr. Otto Warburg was certainly not an author of the last decade, but his findings in the earlier part of the 20th century support what these authors are saying. The two-time Nobel prize winner stated in his book *The Metabolism of Tumors* that "The primary cause of cancer was the replacement of oxygen in the respiratory cell chemistry by the fermentation of glucose." The human cell prefers to function aerobically, that is using oxygen. Fungus and cancer cells function anaerobically, that is without oxygen using fermentation. In 1931 Dr. Warburg received his Nobel prize for this discovery. Fungus and cancer cells not only create acid as the anaerobic cell gives off lactic acid as its waste, but they also thrive in an acid environment. "Cancer is a dark thing living in an acidic place devoid of oxygen."

CURRENT MEDICAL CANCER TREATMENTS

Chemotherapy Reassessed

Professor Gianfranco Valse Pantellini in the treatise interview 'The Individual, Disease and Medicine' says this of chemotherapy: "It has a devastating action on the whole organism . . . it is based on an axiom—rather than a paradox . . . that which causes cancer cures it. Look at what level of absurdity we managed to get to . . ." [9]

A quote from Dr. Simoncini's book states;

> *Chemotherapy in fact destroys everything and how it can make the fungi mass regress is still a mystery. It is a given fact that it dramatically*

exhausts the cells of the marrow and of the blood, thus allowing a greater spreading of the infection.
It irreversibly intoxicates the liver, thus preventing it from building new elements of defence, and it mercilessly knocks out nerve cells, thus weakening the organisms' reactive capabilities and delivering it to the invaders.[10]

Australian Oncologists

In March 2006, an important paper was published in the journal *Clinical Oncology* entitled 'The Contribution of Cytotoxic Chemotherapy to 5-year Survival in Adult Malignancies.' This paper set out to accurately quantify and assess the actual benefit conferred by chemotherapy in the treatment of adults with the most common types of cancer. Although the paper has attracted some attention in Australia, the native country of the paper's authors, it has been greeted with complete silence by the rest of the world.

All three of the paper's authors are oncologists. Lead author Associate **Professor Graeme Morgan** is a radiation oncologist at Royal North Shore Hospital in Sydney; **Professor Robyn Ward** is a medical oncologist at University of New South Wales and Saint Vincent's Hospital. Professor Ward is also a member of the Therapeutic Goods Authority of the Australian Federal Departments of Health and Ageing, the official body that advises the Australian Government on the suitability and efficacy of drugs to be listed on the national Pharmaceutical Benefits Schedule (PBS). The third author, **Doctor Michael Barton**, is a radiation oncologist and a member of the Collaboration for Cancer Outcomes Research and Evaluation, Liverpool Health Service, Sydney, Australia.

The conclusion of these oncologists meticulous study was based on an analysis of the results of all the randomised, controlled clinical trials (RCTs) performed in Australia and the US that reported a statistically significant increase in 5-year survival due to the use of chemotherapy in adult malignancies. Survival data were drawn from the Australian cancer registries and the US National Cancer Institute's Surveillance Epidemiology and End Results (SEER) registry spanning the period January 1990 until January 2004.

Wherever data were uncertain, the authors deliberately erred on the side of overestimating the benefit of chemotherapy. Even so, the study concluded that overall, chemotherapy contributes just over 2 percent to improved survival in cancer patients.

Radiotherapy

Radiotherapy aims to literally burn out the cancer cells, but it is very difficult to effect a mortal blow to the cancer without damaging surrounding tissues and organs. Damaged tissues are always a target for opportunistic fungus. Radiotherapy is not addressing the cause, although it may initially regress cancer growth, radiotherapy can actually create the very environment for cancer to flourish.

Surgery

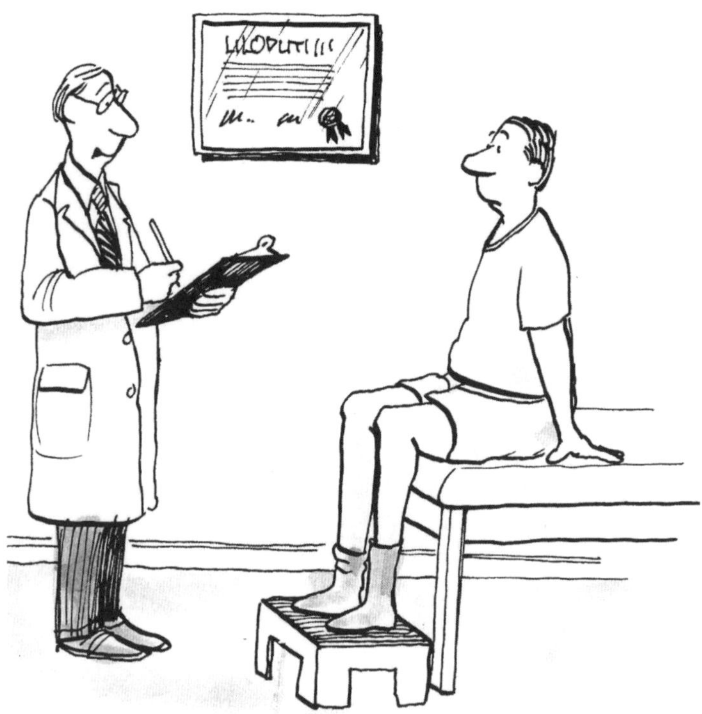

THE GOOD NEWS IS THAT THE CHEMOTHERAPY WORKED AS I EXPECTED, THE BAD NEWS IS I EXPECTED IT WOULDN'T WORK.

Whenever the human body is cut, it is damaged, thus again creating a fruitful environment for fungal increase. Dr. Simoncini found that in a few cases, when the tumour is extremely large and able to be safely removed and the area washed with sodium bicarbonate, there can be benefit.

However, the body has been designed to heal itself, and if the tumour has not reached the point of blocking any major body functions, then given the right conditions, the tumour may be able to be reduced and eliminated.

CONCLUSION

These toxic treatments do not address the root causes of cancer. They are dangerous approaches involving risks. Common sense speaks to us that a treatment that burns, poisons and slashes the human body is contrary to the body's inbuilt healing mechanisms. We are morally and ethically obligated to search out and investigate alternatives that work with the healing powers that are inherent in the human body. In the future, perhaps the current trend of cancer treatments will be looked back on as barbaric as what we now consider blood letting.

Chapter Six References

1. Simoncini T (2007), *Cancer is a Fungus: A Revolution in Tumor Therapy,* Second edition, Edizioni, page 120.
2. ibid. page 142.
3. For more information or to contact Dr. Simoncini visit: <www.cancerfungus.com> or email: <t.simoncini@alice.it>.
4. Madhaven TV, and Gopalan C. "The effect of dietary protein on carcinogenesis of aflatoxin." Arch. Path. 85 (1968): pages 133-137.
5. Youngman LD, and Campbell TC. "Inhibition of aflatoxin B1-induced gamma-glutamyl transpeptidase positive (GGT+) hepatic preneoplastic foci and tumors by low protein diets: evidence that altered GGT+ foci indicate neoplastic potential." Carcinogenesis 13 (1992): pages 1607-1613.
6. Youngman LD. The growth and development of aflatoxin B1-induced preneoplastic lesions, tumors, metastasis, and spontaneous tumors as they are influenced by dietary protein level, type and intervention. Ithaca, NY: Cornell University PhD Thesis, (1990).
7. LeWine HE (2023) "How much protein do you need every day?" *Harvard Health Publishing*, June 22, 2023.
8. Kim H, Caulfield LE, Rebholz CM. (2018) "Healthy Plant-Based Diets Are Associated with Lower Risk of All-Cause Mortality in US Adults." *Journal of Nutrition*. Vol 148, Issue 4, April 2018, pages 624-631.
9. Andromeda, Bologna, 3rd edition, (October 1995).
10. Simoncini, op cit, page 138.

—CHAPTER SEVEN—

The role of Genes in Disease

Are we in bondage to defective genes?

Do genes cause disease? What role does genetics play in causing disease? Let us begin by having a look at what genes are.

Deep inside the cell of every human being, in the tiny nucleus, there is an enormous library of information. This information consists of three thousand million genetic 'letters' called the human genome, or inherited material. The storage unit is the double stranded DNA (deoxyribonucleic acid). The storage capacity is enormous. It is here that the 23 human chromosome pairs make 46 chromosomes. Every gene occurs twice, one from the mother, and one from the father. As the 100,000 inherited characteristics or genes are shared among 23 chromosomes, each chromosome is made up of about 4,400 genes. The total length of the DNA strand, if it could be pulled out, is around 2 metres.

The stored information contains the codes for the development of the smallest structures such as the energy unit inside the cell, the mitochondria, as well as for building the large organs, such as the heart and the liver. The DNA is an incredibly complex design which still baffles scientists today.

Not only the anatomy and physiology of the human frame, but also our numerous talents and predispositions are encoded here, such as music, art, language aptitude and so on.

The exact instructions required for each cell to carry out its allotted task of function, repair and regeneration is contained in our 100,000 genes.

Ribonucleic acid (RNA) is the active agent that carries out the DNA's instructions. DNA transfers its messages accurately to the RNA, which becomes the go-between to specify the amino acid sequence of a protein. This is how the next cell is made under the instruction of the DNA, via the messenger, RNA, whether it is a kidney cell or a liver cell or a brain cell.

In 1953 the headlines in the newspaper proclaimed, 'Secret of Life Discovered!' Watson and Crick had been able to unravel the structure and function of the DNA molecule. The secret code to produce the new cell had been cracked! This discovery led Francis Crick to create biology's 'Central Dogma', the belief that DNA rules. Now many of mankind's problems were blamed on the genes!

But, within the last decade, many researchers are coming up with some compelling evidence that decidedly challenges this theory. The evidence is mounting that reveals the environment—nutritional, spiritual, emotional and mental—affects gene expression. This is good news! We are not locked into the blueprint of the genetic code contained in our genes. Thus it is often quoted, "Genetics loads the gun, but lifestyle pulls the trigger." Some scientists are now claiming that only 2 percent of diseases can be blamed on the genes.

Research regarding the development of the genetic code is showing that influences, while the unborn child's DNA is developing in the womb, are affecting the genetics more than inherited information.

Dr. Thomas Verny in his book *The Secret Life of the Unborn Child*, published in 1981, states that the influence of the parents starts before the child is born. Though the scientific evidence was impressive, the 'experts' were sceptical. The evidence is now gaining momentum. In 1998, David Chamberlain's book, *The Mind of Your Newborn Baby,* showed that the foetal nervous system contains an enormous potential for sensory and learning. Dr. Peter Nathanielsz also published his book, *Life in the Womb; The Origin of Health and Disease* (1999). He sheds further light on the subject. "There is mounting evidence that programming of lifetime health by the conditions in the womb is equally, if not more important, than our genes in determining how we perform mentally and physically through life."

Dr. Daniel J. Siegel in *The Developing Mind* (1999) writes: "For the growing brain of a young child, the social world supplies the most important experiences influencing the expression of genes, which determines how neurons connect to one another in creating the neuronal pathways which give rise to mental activity."

Considering this information, it is not surprising that many health professionals today are looking at health from the cellular level. If the DNA is damaged, the cell will be incapable of reproducing a healthy cell. If the DNA is without the basic building blocks or ingredients it needs to reproduce a healthy cell, then the new cell will not be well!

Let us now consider what damages the cell, thus the DNA, and then we will have a look at the cell's basic requirements for functioning and the ramifications of a deficiency in one or more of these nutrients. To conclude, we will

I CAN'T HELP BEING FAT, IT'S IN MY GENETIC CODE.

consider some 'superfoods' which contain generous amounts of the nutrients required to regenerate and restore damaged DNA.

DAMAGE

A drop in oxygen levels causes the DNA structure to become very susceptible to breakage. Dr. Linus Pauling found that cancer was caused by a broken gene that resulted because of a lack of oxygen in the cell. Lack of oxygen may be caused by many factors:

- breathing low oxygenated air (mould, smog)
- lack of exercise
- chemical poisoning
- heavy metal poisoning (mercury, lead, arsenic, cadmium)
- gastric dysfunction (the inability to effectively digest food)
- deficiency of vitamin B12, iron and copper, as all greatly reduce the red blood cells' ability to carry oxygen.

Environmental Poisons are huge today with barely a spot on the planet not affected. These poisons range from machinery by-products to chemicals on food and toxic household cleaning products. In his book, *Is Your House Making You Sick?,* Dr. Dingle discusses the effect of these household poisons. Dr. Dingle also reveals how fungus can develop and spread in a house. Environmental poisons and fungus are capable of causing damage in the DNA.

Xenoestrogens can also be included in the environmental poisons. These estrogen mimickers, which are found in most environmental toxins and the oral contraceptive pill, are responsible for some mutations in the DNA.

Alcohol is a killer at the cellular level. It is well known that alcohol kills brain cells and it also damages DNA. This is evidenced in children born with Foetal Alcohol Syndrome.

The 4000 chemicals contained in one cigarette cause damage to the DNA structure. Research has shown children of parents who smoke are born with less alveoli in their lungs.

Genetically Modified Food produce proteins that the DNA does not recognise and so is unable to use these proteins in the reproduction of a new cell. The result is mutated cells.

Acid pH Enviroment at the cellular level can result in breakages in the DNA strands. How this can be controlled is discussed in another chapter.

Toxic Emotions can damage the structure of the DNA. In his book, *The Biology of Belief*, Bruce Lipton, PhD, describes how emotions can be toxic to our health. He shows how we are not locked into our genetic patterns, but our genetics are dramatically altered by environmental factors, even in the womb! Our beliefs, our emotions are all part of the environment by which we, our cells, our DNA, are affected. Hate, fear, anxiety, discontent, guilt and distrust, have the ability to cause damage at a cellular level.

DNA Nutrients

The outer upright structure of the DNA is made from polysaccharides.

Polysaccharides are found in all complex carbohydrates. This includes wholegrains, root vegetables and fruits.

The rungs that span across from side to side are made from amino acids (nucleotides). The food source that contains the most efficient burning proteins is legumes (lentils, chickpeas, soy beans and so on), nuts and seeds.

The rungs are attached to the upright polysaccharide structure by minerals. Vegetables are the food group containing the highest amount of minerals, dark green leafy vegetables being notably higher than any other.

Most mutations appear to be a result of mineral deficiencies.

A deficiency in one or two minerals causes a mutation in the DNA. When this mutation occurs, the message that the DNA gives to the RNA is also faulty. This explains why arthritic cells and irritable bowel cells, to name just a few, continue to be made. The RNA must have the necessary minerals to complete the protein.

THE MAIN CAUSES OF MINERAL DEFICIENCIES

Impoverished Soils

The 1992 Earth Summit soil mineral depletion report showed soil depletion in North America to be at 85 percent, the highest in the world, and in the last 30 years these statistics have not improved. This is caused by overtaxing the soil by not alternating crops and also not giving the soil regular rests. Soil is often not fed between crops. Superphosphate is used to attain quick lush growth from the phosphorus, but the plant sadly lacks important minerals, because superphosphate kills the microbes in the soil that are responsible for delivering the minerals to the plants. The high phosphorus levels in the food results in a drop in calcium and magnesium.

Herbicides, Insecticides and Pesticides

With deficiencies in the soil, the plant becomes deficient and in its malnourished state becomes susceptible to disease. Next the farmer brings in the chemicals to kill the bugs that are eating the plant. Now the plants are not only lacking the basic nutrients, resulting in mineral deficient food that is unable to supply the basic requirements for the DNA to reproduce another healthy cell, but they also contain poisons that can contribute to further damage at the DNA level.

Dehydration contributes to mineral deficiency by causing the kidneys to excrete calcium.

Caffeine not only dehydrates the body, but also leaches calcium and magnesium, and is an antagonist to the neurotransmitter, adenosine. Adenosine is needed for RNA synthesis (function).

GOOD NEWS!

The human body has the ability to heal itself. It will heal itself if given the right conditions. Especially the right nutrition.

Minerals are essential. Lack of minerals is the number one cause of DNA mutations. Organic food is no longer an option but a must. Organic gardening ensures the soil is well-fed, and the microbes that break down the minerals in the soil making them available for the plant are nurtured by composting. The result is food that contains all the necessary minerals for proper functioning DNA.

SUPER FOODS

There are foods that have exceptional properties to bring about a healing condition. The foods with these properties are very high in minerals and some are passed by as being a pest—often pulled out, burnt or poisoned. It is because of their wide range and exceptionally high content of minerals that they are so beneficial in reversing illness through supplying the essential and missing components at the DNA level.

Following are some herbs that have been naturally designed to boost the healing powers of the body.

Stinging nettle: This plant is able to pull more minerals out of the soil than any other plant. In many European countries it is prized as a miracle food. Isabell Shipard in her book, *How can I use Herbs in my Daily Life?*, gives an excellent description of stinging nettle and it's impressive array of minerals and vitamins: Iron, calcium, magnesium, potassium, manganese, selenium, silicon, sodium, zinc, copper, chlorine, sulphur, chromium, iodine, Vitamins A,B,C,D,E and K.

Stinging nettle is known to build red blood cells because of its very high chlorophyll content. Chlorophyll is almost identical in molecular structure to human blood. As a result, it aids in the delivery of oxygen through the body.

But how do we eat it?

A tea can be made by pouring boiling water onto the leaves, let sit for ten minutes and strain, or the leaves can be cooked like spinach. (Handy hint: use leather gloves when collecting and chopping!) Stinging nettle can also be added to other vegetables when making a juice.

Aloe Vera: This wonder plant is well known and easily grown.

Aloe vera also contains a very impressive line-up of minerals and vitamins: Vitamins B1, B2, B3, B6,

B9 (folic acid), B12, A, C and Minerals including calcium, zinc, chromium, magnesium, potassium, sodium, manganese, chlorine, copper, phosphorous, sulphur, silicon, iron, cobolt and boron. It is a polysaccharide.

Aloe vera also contains two monoatomic elements—iridium and rhodium. These two elements are beginning to receive a lot of attention as they appear to be able to directly aid in the restoration of damaged or mutated DNA structures.

Aloe vera can be added to vegetable juice. Use the clear gel, which is revealed once the skin is peeled away. Up to two dessertspoons daily is recommended to assist DNA healing.

Comfrey: Comfrey also contains iridium and rhodium and Vitamins B1, B2, B3, B5, B6, B12, Minerals including calcium, phosphorus, cobolt, magnesium, potassium, iron, sulphur, manganese, sodium, chromium, copper, boron, lead, zinc and selenium.

Comfrey leaves can be added to vegetable juices or finely chopped and sprinkled through salads.

Super Emotions: Just as important as the super foods are super emotions. Love, tenderness, mercy, joy, peace, gentleness and compassion are emotions that have the ability to bring restoration and healing at a cellular level. These emotions are designed to heal.

MINERALS IN THE HUMAN GENOME

To illustrate the importance of minerals let us have a look at how many times each appears in the human genome (the genetic information contained in the DNA).

- **Aluminium:** 23 million (excess is toxic, the antidote is the chemical element yttrium, found in lettuce);
- **Cobolt:** 19 million (the central molecule of B12, holds the DNA strands together);
- **B12:** 18.8 million (deficiency causes DNA breakages which results in cellular mutations);
- **Sodium:** 18 million (keeps calcium mobile, main transport vehicle of nutrients from food to liver);
- **Lithium:** 17 million (the work horse of our emotions);
- **Silica:** 17 million (controls ovarian DNA, highest source is cucumber);
- **Boron:** 15.2 million (activates vitamin D and controls 229 genes);
- **Potassium:** 15 million (necessary for proper heart function and the sodium/potassium cellular pump);
- **Sulphur:** 12 million (essential for cartilage, also liver detoxification);
- **Chlorine:** 11 million (component of stomach digestive enzymes);
- **Magnesium:** 11 million (major mineral in tumour-suppressing genes; antidote for phosphorus overload);
- **Phosphorus:** 8 million (an essential mineral for DNA function, but excess will deplete magnesium stores);
- **Selenium:** 2 million (essential for stabilising the double strands of the tumour-suppressing genes; the CEO for iron, copper, and zinc; this mineral also detoxifies mercury, lead, arsenic and cadmium).

We do not have a number for presence in the human genome for the following minerals, but they are as equal in importance:

- **Carbon:** The carbon content is high in vitamin C and protects against disease. Carbon and selenium work closely together;
- **Nitrogen:** Nitrogen as used in the form of protein;

- **Chromium:** The CEO for sugar regulation in the body; works closely with insulin.
- **Manganese:** Used in the brain for memory recall, essential for nerve function;
- **Iron:** A deficiency is often because of low levels of copper, B12 and vitamin C. Iron is a major component of the red blood cells;
- **Copper:** Used by the DNA to form the tumour-suppressing gene p53, used by the joints as elastin. A deficiency in copper can cause hyperthyroidism;
- **Zinc:** Essential for reproduction and immunity, and works with copper;
- **Molybdenum:** Prevents the formation of uric acid crystals (gout), used in detoxification; safeguards DNA strands;
- **Iodine:** Essential for thyroid function and the immune system; regulates temperature.

HONEY—I'VE FOUND A SOLUTION FOR YOUR IRON DEFICIENCY

ORBITALLY REARRANGED MONATOMIC ELEMENTS (ORMES)

Sea water contains all the minerals that the body needs, and in the right balance. This is why sea water is called an isotonic solution. Many of these elements are present in an Orbitally Rearranged Monatomic form (ORMES). What this means is that these minerals or elements have changed their state and now exhibit superconductivity higher than their commonly found state.

A process has been developed that causes the ORMES to 'drop out' of the sea water while the remaining salty water is removed. The remaining colloidal elements (ORMES) are present in a white cloud-like suspended form. The white liquid is alkaline and stable in nature and is easily assimilated by the human body. ORMES can produce a detox reaction so it is recommended to begin with a couple of drops under the tongue and slowly increase. Consult your health professional for dosage.

The monatomic elements, rhodium and iridium, are receiving attention today as having the ability to repair DNA damage. A major pharmaceutical company in the US, BMS, has found that these ORMES interact with the human DNA to correct and perfect the structure.

- Sea water has 175,000 ppb dissolved solids and has a pH of around 7.5.
- ORMES have 5200 dissolved ppb solids with a pH of around 10.75.

Foods with the highest content of rhodium and iridium are aloe vera, almond, apricot seed, flaxseed, sheep sorrel, carrots and blood root. These plants must be grown in organic, mineral-rich soils.

Our DNA and RNA would literally fall apart without minerals, which effectively glue the amino acid bands (nucleotides) to the walls of the DNA structure, which are made up of polysaccharides.

—CHAPTER EIGHT—

Fuel for Life

Food performs or deforms

The human body has been designed to heal itself. It is a self-cleansing, self-healing organism. The human body will heal itself, if given the right conditions. We will now consider one of the most important conditions —the right fuel.

One of Hippocrates' most quoted statements is: "Let food be your medicine, and medicine be your food."

This makes a lot of sense when one considers that the food we eat is broken down into microscopic particles that are absorbed into the bloodstream and eventually reach every cell in our body. Our ingested food is the cell's fuel. The fact is, we are just a bunch of cells, so the nutritional status of every cell basically determines the health of the body, and the nutritional status of each cell is determined by the food we eat!

Food that is grown in mineral-rich soil, is mineral rich. Their mineral wealth is due to the microorganisms that release these minerals from the soil into the plant. This food contains all the nourishment the cell needs.

Common agriculture habits that deplete the soil of their minerals by growing the same crops repeatedly, year after year without replenishing the soil with compost, results in impoverished soils which results in impoverished plants, the end product being impoverished people!

The resulting impoverished plants are unable to resist disease, and so now the farmer must spray his crop with poisonous sprays so that they may survive. The plant is now not only nutrient deficient but is laden with toxic chemicals!

Add to this long refrigeration and overcooking, and by the time most food reaches the table it is almost totally inadequate to supply even the most basic needs of each cell in the body. No wonder many bodies are not able to heal! Organically grown food is becoming essential rather than optional. But there's more.

There are three essential nutrients required by the human body for life. They are **fibre, protein and fat.** Essential means the body cannot make it, so it must be added to the diet.

The following three food groups—**fibre, protein and fat**—also keep the food in the stomach longer.

This is necessary to:

1. Ensure a consistent, regular, steady release of glucose to every cell in the body.
2. Give the stomach the essential 3–4 hours needed to digest the food, followed by an hour of rest. This stomach rest is a vital component of digestion, because it is here that the gastric glands replace the enzymes needed for the next meal.
3. Prevent the unnecessary, expensive and time-consuming pastime of continual eating.

FIBRE

When considering fibre, one is also considering the vitamins (vital for life), and minerals (mini-components of life). The food with the highest fibre content is vegetables; they are also the highest source of minerals. Minerals make up the basic components of the body, but they cannot function without vitamins. These two essential nutrients are necessary for every chemical reaction in the body, often called catalysts. Fibre is also found in wholegrains, fruit, legumes, seeds and nuts. Fibre is needed by the gastrointestinal tract to stimulate peristalsis and sweep the many little curves and corners found there. The house needs its daily sweep; fibre is the broom. A fact not realised by many, is that the refining of grains to remove the fibre can also remove up to 80 percent of the vitamins.

PROTEIN

Protein is an essential nutrient. The nucleus of every cell in the body (with the exception of the red blood cell which contains no nucleus) contains the DNA that is programmed to repair. The DNA requires amino acids to do the repair. Amino acids are the product of protein breakdown. No protein, no repair!

A person on a low- or no-protein diet cannot heal. The energy cycle inside every cell requires one or two or more different amino acids for every chemical reaction, and there are about 13 of them! Low protein diets may be the cause of low energy.

Every cell in the body is surrounded by a membrane, and this membrane is made up of 50 percent protein and 50 percent fat.

Vegetarian protein is found chiefly in the seed. The seed is the reproductive part of the plant. To be able to reproduce itself the seed must contain all the essential amino acids or life could not come out of the seed. The book, *Nutrition Almanac*, shows that the 'seeds' contain all the essential amino acids required for all cell molecular functions.

There are four groups of seed:

- **Grains:** wheat, rye, spelt, barley, oats, millet, quinoa, buckwheat, amaranth.
- **Legumes:** lentils, chickpeas, kidney beans, soybeans, black eyed beans, lima beans, split peas.
- **Nuts:** almonds, brazil, pecans, macadamia, cashews, hazelnuts, walnuts.
- **Seeds:** pepita (pumpkin seeds), sunflower, flaxseed, sesame, chia.

FAT

Every cell in the body is surrounded by a lipid membrane. Lipid is a form of fat. As previously mentioned, this membrane is composed of 50 percent fat and 50 percent protein. The joints need to be oiled, our eyes, hair, skin, in fact every part of our body needs to be oiled! The sex hormones and stress hormones in our bodies are made from cholesterol, which is another form of fat in our body. A large component of the brain is fat.

The standard American diet (SAD) is sadly flawed.

Fat phobia has taken over the nation. This has caused the SAD diet to become even sadder. Carbohydrates are now the reigning king as people have rushed to this food group in an endeavour to escape the so-called evils of fat. Current figures show that 73 percent of Americans, and 63.8 percent or Brits have obesity or are overweight, and this is on the low-fat diet!

One reason that has caused nutritionists to advise people to lower their fat consumption is that fat burns at 9 calories per gram, whereas glucose burns at 4 per gram. The misconception about calories has risen from a lack of understanding as to what a calorie is. A calorie is a unit of energy. If a person wanted a high energy food what should they eat? Fat! But if more units of energy are consumed than will be burnt, then it stands to reason that the body will store it as fat.

Three points of consideration at this point. Fats can be overdone, and there are fats that heal and there are fats that can kill.

First we will discuss the killer fats and then we will look at the fats that heal.

> Three points of consideration . . . Fats can be overdone, and there are fats that heal and there are fats that can kill.

KILLER FATS

1) Most toxins are found to be fat soluble and so are found in the fat of animals. I do not believe that animals or their products can be considered safe, and one of the reasons is the exposure to the environmental toxins and the resulting storage in their bodies, especially the areas of fat.

2) Refined sugars and refined carbohydrates are virtually totally deficient in fibre, and so glucose is released quickly into the bloodstream. This rapid rise of glucose demands a corresponding release of high insulin from the pancreas in an attempt to balance blood glucose levels. To get these glucose levels back to normal, insulin facilitates the delivery of glucose into the cell.

But on a high carbohydrate diet there is a high residue of glucose left over. To solve this problem, the liver stores a small amount as glycogen (quick-release glucose stores) and the remaining excess glucose is stored as fat! This means that the 'fat-free' product, which is usually high in refined sugars in an attempt to make it palatable, is stored as a far more dangerous fat.

3) Heat alters the molecular structure of fats. When the molecular structure of fats changes it becomes mutenogenic, or cancer-forming. The two most common ways this is seen today is in fried foods and margarine. The frying of

foods is self-explanatory. The process of converting liquid oils, or polyunsaturated oils, into solid margarine also changes the molecular structure of fats. All margarines are saturated fats; if they weren't, they would be liquid! But that's not all. In the process of producing a solid, 'spreadable' butter alternative, we now have a product that is one molecular structure short of plastic. The cells do not recognise this. It fits nowhere and causes untold havoc and damage everywhere.

HEALING FATS

Healing fats can be put into three categories.

1. Polyunsaturated fats

Omega 3 and omega 6 are essential fatty acids (EFAs), so-called because they are essential to human health. Animals cannot put these EFAs into their fatty acid chains. Only plants are able to create these EFAs, and so they must be taken into the body via food. They are found in a variety of plant foods, particularly some seeds and nuts.

Our body uses unsaturated fats and EFAs to construct, maintain and repair the membranes that surround every cell in the body. The electrical system in the brain is dependent upon an adequate supply of these essential oils.

These highly unsaturated fatty acids attract oxygen, help generate electrical currents, and so help transform light energy into electrical energy, and then into nerve impulses.

In the omega 3 (O_3) family, there are two omega 3s called Eicosapentaenoic acid (EPA) and Docosahexaenoic acid (DHA), found in cold water fish and other northern marine animals. These fish are high in omega 3 because of the red algae they eat.

Another member of the omega 3 family is alphalineolenic acid (ALA), found in flaxseed, chia, hemp, walnut and soybean.

Of the omega 3 family, the most unsaturated fatty acid is DHA. In the body, 25 percent of the brain is DHA, 40 percent of the cortical grey matter, and 90 percent of the fatty acid in the retina is all DHA.

From this omega 3 family, the body is able to convert ALA to the more active and more unsaturated fatty acid, EPA. The body then converts EPA into DHA.

In fish, the ALA is converted to EPA, then to DHA, which means the DHA is readily available to the body in fish oil.

But the bad news is that many of the fish with the highest amounts of DHA and EPA, such as tuna, are contaminated with high levels of dioxin, mercury and PCBs (toxic chlorinated hydro-carbons).

Thus, a far more desirable way to provide your body with these vital oils is through seeds and nuts, as ALA. ALA is the precursor to EPA and DHA. The human body is able to convert ALA, through several stages, to EPA, and then to DHA.

As many as 95% of people do not get enough DHA and EPA, one of the possible reasons is the damaging effect of sugar, stress, alcohol, many medication (such as aspirin) and high levels of trans fatty acids (found in fast foods). These factors tend to reduce DHA production by *blocking* the primary enzymes that convert ALA to DHA.

Polyunsaturated fats spoil easily and so are best eaten in their natural state.

Sources

The foods that are highest in omega 3 (ALA) are flaxseed (linseed), chia seed, sunflower seeds, pepita (pumpkin seeds), hemp seed, walnuts and soybeans. There is a small amount in olives and olive oil.

2. Monounsaturated Fats

Almonds and olives are the highest source of monounsaturated fat. All other nuts and seeds contain small amounts. Our bodies can manufacture saturated and monounsaturated fats from other foods. Monounsaturated fats are not as susceptible to damage as polyunsaturated fats.

3. Saturated Fats

The fat in our bodies consists of 45 percent saturated, 50 percent monounsaturated, and 5 percent polyunsaturated. Considering this, it is clear that our bodies need over ten times the saturated and monounsaturated fat as it does polyunsaturated fat. Saturated fat is a vital nutrient. It provides an important source of energy for the body and is essential for the absorption of vitamins and minerals. Saturated fat is required for proper growth and repair, also maintenance of all body tissues. This fat is a very stable fat, unlike mono and poly unsaturated fats. The main sources of saturated fat are found in animal fats, butter, palm oil and coconut oil. With the danger of spoiling and high risk of contamination from environmental poisons with animal fats, I advise using coconut oil. Dr. Bruce Fife has written several books that explain the amazing health benefits of coconut oil.

WHAT ABOUT CARBOHYDRATES?

Never in the history of mankind have human beings consumed so many carbohydrates! Down on the farm, the carbohydrates are the slow foods, all requiring an amount of time to prepare, such as potatoes, pasta, rice, cereal, bread, cakes and biscuits.

However in the city, these foods are the fast ones! They are found in every fast food shop, easily found in every town.

It is estimated that 84 percent of the UK population currently live in cities, compared to 1950 when the population living in UK cities was 79%. That figure is set to rise to 92.2% by 2030.[1] These statistics help to explain why western countires have become such high carbohydrate consumers. It's fast, easy food!

In light of how the body deals with the excess glucose produced on a high carbohydrate diet, is it not surprising that diagnoses of diabetes in the UK have doubled over the past 15 years. As of 2021 almost 4.1 million people in the UK have diabetes, with predictions that one in 10 adults in the UK could have diabetes by 2030.[2] One can appreciate the extra demands on the pancreas with such a high carbohydrate intake.

With the information explaining how the excess glucose stores as fat, it is clear why over 63% of adults aged 18 years and over in England are overweight or living with obesity.[3]

Even scarier is the realisation of how the high carbohydrate diet, with its high glucose delivery to the blood, is supplying cancer cells with their favourite fuel—and at a high rate! Heart disease is the leading cause of death for men, women, and people of most racial and ethnic groups in the United States.[4]

Carbohydrates, therefore, need to be viewed as the negotiating part of the meal. They do not necessarily need to be eliminated but seriously reviewed.

Our consumption of carbohydrates will change depending on our size, height, weight, age, fitness, physical activity, mental activity and health.

Gluten

The two most popular grains consumed in the United Kingdom are wheat and oats. These grains are high in gluten, much higher than other grains. Over the last 50 years coeliac disease and other gluten-related disorders have increased, affecting at least 1 in every 100 people in the UK,[5] this profound rise cannot be fully explained by improved serological techniques or better recognition by physicians. I believe there are four reasons for this increase:

1. Western Lifestyle diets are high in gluten, such as cereal and toast for breakfast, sandwiches for lunch, pasta for dinner, with cakes and biscuits in between.
2. In 1968 Mexico, Pakistan and India started to export a new hybridised wheat. This grain was developed by Dr. Norman Borlaug for the Cooperative Wheat Research Production Program, a joint venture by the Rockefeller Foundation and the Mexican government. Hybridised wheat is much shorter, but has a far higher yield, it also contains a very complex gluten or protein structure, which produces a far more elastic grain ensuring that pasta holds together nicely and bread and cakes can bend without breaking making it very popular. Today, 99 percent of wheat is from this hybridised grain. While Borlaug received a Nobel Prize for his lifetime work to feed a hungry world, it appears his hybrid grain with it's complex gluten structure is far more difficult for the human body to digest.

3. Babies are introduced to grains before they are able to digest them properly. The first teeth that appear in a baby's mouth are the four at the front top, and the four at the bottom front. These teeth are tearing teeth, and thus are well designed to handle fruit and vegetables. Seven to ten months is the average age these teeth appear. Next, the first four molars come through, this happens between fourteen and twenty-two months of age. These large four cusped teeth are for grinding—grinding grain. As these teeth emerge the glands in the mouth begin to release ptylin, which is the enzyme that is essential for the effective digestion of starch. When babies are given starch before these molars are present, malabsorption syndrome in the gut can develop, which often manifests itself as gluten intolerance in later years.
4. The majority of wheat grown in the world today is grown in soils that are fertilised with superphosphate. Superphosphate kills the micro organisms in the soil that are responsible for releasing the minerals from the soil and making them available to the roots of the plant. As a result the plant becomes mineral deficient. These minerals are necessary for the effective digestion and absorption of the gluten in the wheat.

Considering the above information, it is wise to ensure that we include in our daily food program substantial fibre, adequate protein, sufficient fat, and add the carbohydrates (ideally gluten free) as the age, size, height, fitness, health, physical and mental demands require.

Chapter Eight References

1 "Percentage of global population living in cities, by continent." *The Guardian*, <https://www.theguardian.com/news/datablog/2009/aug/18/percentage-population-living-cities> accessed December 2023.

2 Lacobucci G. (2021) "One in 10 UK adults could have diabetes by 2030, warns charity" *British Medical Journal*, 2021; 375 :n2453 doi:10.1136/bmj.n2453.

3 Obesity Profile: Short statistical commentary May 2023 < https://www.gov.uk/government/statistics/obesity-profile-update-may-2023/obesity-profile-short-statistical-commentary-may-2023>.

4 Heart Disease Facts, *CDC National Division for Heart Disease and Stroke Prevention*, Updated May 15, 2023 <https://www.cdc.gov/heartdisease/facts.htm>.

5 Al Toma A, Volta U, Aurrcchio R et al. (2019) "European Society for the Study of Coeliac Disease guideline for for Coeliac Disease & other Gluten-Related Disorders." United Eur Gastro Journal 2019; 7 (5): 583-613

—CHAPTER NINE—

Conquering Candida

and other fungus/yeast-related problems

In this chapter we are going to show how to conquer fungus/yeast-related problems in the body. We have established how it can enter the body, and how many and varied the symptoms can be. The following program is the basics. Each person will do their own individual fine-tuning; age, fitness, environment, health status and the severity of the condition need to be taken into consideration. It is yours to design a self-healing program that will work for you.

The most powerful way to conquer candida, fungus and yeast outbreaks in the body is to take the three-pronged approach.

1) Starve the fungus.

2) Kill the fungus.

3) Restore the balance of the beneficial microbes.

1) STARVE THE FUNGUS

The favourite food of fungus is sugar and yeast. In order to starve the fungus, these must be completely eliminated from the diet.

- **Sugars:** All sugars must be removed from the diet, particularly cane and beet sugar in all of its forms. Honey and all other sweeteners including fruits and fruit juices must be eliminated. This will deprive the fungus of its most effective fuel. Granny Smith apples and grapefruit are the exception, as these fruits have a lower sugar content and contain antifungal properties. The grapefruit seed contains phytochemicals that are potent fungus killers.
- **Yeast:** All yeast must be removed from the diet. Yeasted bread (this does not include sourdough bread, which contains Lactobacillus bacteria), all alcoholic beverages, yeast spreads and yeast extracts, brewer's yeast, mushrooms and soy sauce.
- **Old Food:** All cooked food over two days old. Any food that has a trace of mould on it must be discarded. All rice is particularly susceptible to fungal growth and must be eaten freshly cooked.
- **Corn and Wheat:** Corn grain and wheat grain are extremely vulnerable to fungal growth when they are stored. These grains must be eliminated in the initial stages while overcoming a fungal problem in the body.
- **Peanuts:** Peanuts are notorious for fungal infestation and so must be avoided especially in the form of peanut butter.
- **Meat:** Animals are often fed mouldy grains that are declared unfit for human consumption, and this fungus is in the meat. Aside from this, research shows the casein in meat and dairy products has the ability to encourage fungal growth. Aged cheeses and most dairy products commonly show fungal infestation when tested.
- **Environment:** Check that there are no damp and dark areas in your house where mould can flourish. Mulch situated close to a house can also be a source of mould. Be careful of compost bins and mulch when they are at their fungal breakdown stages.

  SBS produced a DVD series in 2007 called *Is your House Killing You?* in which

Dr. Peter Dingle, a Senior Lecturer and Associate Professor at the School of Environmental Science at Murdoch University in WA, covered the stories of nine families who were sick, and in many of the homes there was a mould problem. Dr. Dingle searches for the cause and shows how to remedy the problem. The series is a real eye-opener. He states that bleach kills mould, but feeds fungus, whereas vinegar kills mould *and* fungus.

- **Chemicals:** Eliminate all contact with chemicals. Assess cleaning products, shampoos and conditioners, soap, laundry detergents, and even nylon clothes, especially underwear and night gowns.

- **Heavy Metals:** Fish today are generally unsafe to eat because of contamination with mercury and dioxin, especially the big fish. The bigger the fish, the higher the concentration of mercury.

Amalgam fillings, used in dentistry, can be up to 60 percent mercury. It is recommended that these be removed and replaced with white fillings, which don't contain mercury.

2) KILL THE FUNGUS

The following herbs and foods can assist in bringing yeast under control. The most effective way to use the herbs is to alternate them. Try 2 weeks at a time for each.

Herbs

- **Garlic:** has powerful antifungal properties. When taking garlic to treat Candida, you may experience an adverse, albeit healthy, reaction. This is what is generally referred to as the 'Herxheimer' or 'Die-off' effect. While living in the body, most of the offending microbes somehow manage to evade the body's immune system. However, when exposed to powerful eradicators, large numbers of pathological microbes will die. Soon after, their cell-wall proteins (which are essentially toxins) are absorbed through the weakened mucous membrane. The body then begins its natural processes to get rid of these toxins; however, if toxins exist in numbers too large for the elimination system to handle, you may experience exhaustion and flu-like symptoms. The severity will depend on the extent of your condition, the state of your immune and eliminatory systems, and how much garlic you have consumed. Bring your dose of garlic back to a manageable amount. Garlic in either raw or supplement form is effective.

- **Olive Leaf Extract:** Rich in a phytochemical called Oleuropein, which has a strong antifungal effect.
- **Oregano Oil:** An essential oil, containing some of the most potent antifungal phytochemicals.
- **Pau D'Arco:** A South American herb, contains a phytochemical Lapachol, which is a powerful fungicide.
- **Horopito:** A New Zealand herb, contains potent antifungal properties in the form of Kolorex capsules.
- **Grapefruit Seed Extract:** One of the strongest fungus killers there is.
- **Iodine:** An extremely effective fungicide. Lugol's solution contains iodine and potassium iodide in water at a combined concentration of about 6.5 mg of iodine per drop. Dosage can begin at one drop a day, applied to the skin. The dose can be increased to 6-8 drops several times a day as the body is able.

Alkalise

- **Alkalise:** Another way to kill fungus is to alkalise the body. Fungus thrives in an acid environment, and creates an acid environment. This is how fungus 'feathers its nest'! In the next chapter we will discuss how to create the alkaline environment that fungus hates.

Foods

- **Foods**: The following foods can be added to the daily diet and will give an added boost to the body's ability to conquer fungus as they contain impressive amounts of antifungal plant chemicals.

> As the human body adapts and adjusts to the herbs, it is advised to alternate the herbal medicines, taking each two weeks at a time. This will help the body to remain reactive to the active components in the herbs. It is recommended that a health professional be consulted for specific doses to suit the individual.

- Coconut in all its forms is 40 percent antifungal. Caprylic acid is the fatty acid contained in coconut which is a strong fungicide.
- All legumes, particularly soy, contain antifungal properties.
- All raw nuts and seeds can survive storage or planting only because they contain antifungal properties (except peanuts and pistachio nuts, which are particularly susceptible to fungal growth).
  If seeds didn't contain these fungal-fighting agents, they would never survive storage or planting.

3) RESTORE THE BALANCE

A contributing factor in most fungal problems is an imbalance in the gut flora. The largest amount of microorganisms in the body are found in the gastrointestinal tract. The yeasts and bacteria living in the small and large intestines are extremely beneficial. But only when found in the right balance.

Candida albicans is yeast that exists in the intestines of humans. Lactobacillus Acidophilus and Bifidus bacterium, often called acidophilus and bifidus or the friendly/healthy bacteria, are the two permanent bacteria that inhabit the gastrointestinal tract. These are just three of the four hundred species of indigenous organisms residing there and when in the correct balance, they serve us well.

Drugs, antibiotics, alcohol, refined sugar, stress and unhealthy lifestyle habits have the ability to inhibit and destroy the healthy bacteria. Candida is an opportunistic organism, and in this situation has the ability to multiply out of control, which contributes to a yeast-fungus problem in the body. Part of bringing the correct balance back is to encourage the presence of acidophilus and bifidus.

Cultured foods containing healthy bacteria include sourdough bread, sauerkraut, miso, tofu, tempeh and soy yoghurt.

A probiotic supplement, containing acidophilus and bifidus, is a must to speed up repopulating the gastrointestinal tract with this healthy bacteria. Flood the gastrointestinal tract with the 'good guys' and the 'bad guys' don't have a chance!

THE ANTIFUNGAL FOOD PROGRAM

The food we eat can quite dramatically affect the body's environment. Some foods feed fungus, whereas some foods can create a condition that will deter and even kill fungus.

It is recommended to adhere to **stage one** of the antifungal program for at least one month. After this, **stage two** can be implemented.

The length of time spent on stage two will depend on the severity of the condition. Some who have been battling with yeast/fungal problems for several years find that stage one gives an initial blow to the life of these organisms, and stage two affords an effective maintenance program.

Below is an example of a menu that adheres to the stage one food lists on the following page:

Example of a daily Stage One menu

BREAKFAST	LUNCH	DINNER
• Grapefruit or granny smith apple • Cooked grain (such as millet, rice, quinoa or buckwheat) ADD • Savoury lentils OR • Stewed apples topped with coconut milk or soy yoghurt	• Raw salad with a salad dressing (see recipes on page 153) WITH • Baked potato/sweet potato and steamed carrots and broccoli WITH • *Chickpea Cardamom Casserole* (page 120) PLUS • 8 pecan nuts	• Bowl of *Split Pea Soup* (page 140) AND/OR • A few Ryvita crackers with avocado and tomato

The Antifungal Diet—Stage One

	STAGE 1 FOODS INCLUDED	**STAGE 1** FOODS EXCLUDED
SUGARS	None	Honey, maple syrup, artificial and herbal sweeteners, and all other sugars
FRUIT	Granny Smith apples, grapefruit, lemons, avocado and tomato	All other fruit, including their juices
VEGETABLES	Fresh, unblemished vegetables and their juices	
BEVERAGES	Herb teas, water and unsweetened soymilk	Tea, coffee, fruit juice, cola and fizzy drinks
GRAINS	Freshly cooked brown rice, spelt, sourdough bread, quinoa, amaranth, millet, buckwheat, rye and a small amount of non-wheat or corn pasta	Wheat and corn
LEGUMES	All legumes including soy and soy products	Peanuts
YEAST PRODUCTS	None	Yeasted bread, mushrooms, alcohol and marmite/vegemite
VINEGAR	Black olives in brine permitted	Pickles, salad dressings, soy sauce and green olives
OILS	Extra Virgin olive oil, flaxseed oil and coconut oil	Margarine, corn and peanut oil
NUTS	All raw nuts, including coconut	Peanuts and pistachios
SEEDS	All seeds such as pumpkin, sesame and sunflower	
CULTURED FOODS	Tofu, soy yoghurt, miso, sauerkraut and tempeh	All aged cheeses

The Antifungal Diet—Stage Two

Stage two of the Antifungal Diet is the same as stage one, but with the addition of all berries to the fruit section, and maple syrup and stevia added for sweeteners.

The Cancer-Conquering Diet

This is the diet which enables the body to eliminate cancer. The human body alone has the power to heal itself, and it will heal itself if given the right conditions. This diet is the ultimate formula to bring about a radical change that will cause death to cancer cells. Cancer cells self-destruct when deprived of glucose. It is their favourite food and because a cancer cell consumes 15 times the fuel compared to a healthy cell, it is the first to suffer.

Points to ponder concerning cancer:

- The main cause of cancer is malnutrition at the cellular level.
- A healthy body will not get cancer.
- Exposure to chemicals, poisons, heavy metals, excessive hormones and fungus will not cause cancer if the body has sufficient nutrients to detoxify them and the immune system is working well.

The following food program is recommended for six weeks. It eliminates almost all glucose going into the body, and is designed to give a severe blow to diseased cells by avoiding any excess glucose being available for the diseased cells to grow on. The aim is to reduce glucose levels to as low as possible, as diseased cells grow on sugar. This food program contains the plant protein, the vitamins and minerals, the essential fatty acids and enough carbohydrates to nutritionally support a healing response and to supply all the nutritional requirements for optimal health in the human body.

Foods in the Cancer-Conquering Diet

- **Legumes:** Including lentils, chickpeas, red kidney beans and soybeans. Ensure they are well rinsed, before and while cooking. They also must be cooked until soft. The cooking water needs to be discarded and flavourings added to serve. Culinary herbs aid the digestion of legumes. This section also include, tofu, soy yoghurt and miso.

- **Vegetables:**
  - Asparagus, peas and beans, tomatoes (cooked tomatoes contain lycopene—antifungal), onions, garlic, ginger
  - **Root vegetables:** Potatoes, sweet potato, pumpkin (squash), beetroots, parsnips, carrots, turnips
  - **Green leafy vegetables:** All green leafy vegetables are high in anticancer properties, including celery, and can be eaten raw or lightly steamed. Other examples are fresh herbs such as basil, coriander, oregano, rosemary and parsley, all of which also enhance digestion
  - **Brassica vegetables:** Cabbage, kale, turnip, brussels sprouts, broccoli and cauliflower—lightly steamed. Raw brassicas inhibit thyroid function.

- **Grains:** Brown rice is antifungal if cooked fresh and eaten immediately—or at least the same day. Other grains include millet, buckwheat and quinoa.

- **Fruit:** Avocado, lemon, lime, tomato.

- **Oils:** Olive oil, coconut oil, flax oil and coconut milk.

- **Fresh nuts and seeds:** All raw nuts, including coconut and seeds such as pepita (pumpkin seeds), sesame and sunflower.

- **Additions:**
  - Cayenne pepper
  - Turmeric (high in antifungal properties)
  - Celtic salt (approximately 1–1 ½ teaspoons per day)

- **Supplements**
  - ½ teaspoon vitamin C (must contain the bioflavonoids) 3 times daily with 1 teaspoon of Aloe vera (antifungal)
  - 1 teaspoon vitamin B Complex 2 times daily (This kick-starts normal metabolic function. Reduces toxicity of fungi.)
  - Acidophilus/bifidus—¼ – ½ teaspoon daily, ¾ hour before breakfast, to help restore the healthy bacteria.
  - Mineral supplement—1 teaspoon twice daily
  - Bitter herbs to aid digestion: gentian, dandelion, golden seal, liquorice, ginger
  - A variety of antifungal herbs also need to be taken. It is recommended that these herbs be alternated every fortnight. A list of these are included in the section 'Conquering Candida'
  - Four green drinks daily, between meals.

Example of a Cancer-Conquering Diet

BREAKFAST

- Salad, such as tomato, cucumber, avocado

PLUS

- ½ cup freshly cooked brown rice
- 1 cup *Quick Brown Lentils* (page 118)
- Steamed vegetables
- 8-10 almonds

Lunch

- Salad such as grated carrot/ beetroot, celery, lettuce, olives, avocado, with *Tahini mayo* dressing (page 153)
- Baked potato and pumpkin or sweet potato
- Stir-fry vegetables
- *Lovely Lima Beans* (page 133)
- 6 macadamia nuts

DINNER

- *The Mighty Minestrone Soup* (page 141) or herb tea.

After six weeks on the Cancer-Conquering diet it is advised to move onto stage one of the antifungal program for at least two months then move onto stage two which will be the maintenance program.

A COMMENT ON SOY

The soybean has been eaten in Asia for thousands of years. It is eaten fresh, as a dried legume, as tofu or as soybean milk. The Asians are well known for living long, healthy lives. Part of this can be contributed to soybean consumption but part also to the large amounts of fresh vegetables and fresh water and their active lifestyles, which are relatively free of caffeine, alcohol and sugar. The soybean is non-genetically modified, organically grown and the whole soybean is used.

Dr. Harry Miller, an English surgeon who worked in China for several decades in the early 1800s, pioneered the work in soybean milk. Thousands of Chinese babies' lives were saved with his soybean milk.

There has been much media coverage in the last few years warning us of the dangers of eating soy. It has been linked specifically with hormonal cancers such as breast cancer, uterine cancer, prostate cancer, and the like. There seems to be a great discrepancy between the soybean of the Orient and the soybean in developed countries. It is a fact that the soybean has the most potent

DO YOU THINK I CAN GET SOME OF THE HEALTH BENEFITS OF SOY IF I LOOK AT THIS TOFU WHILE EATING MY HOTDOG?

anticancer properties of any plant on planet earth. It is twice as high in protein as any other legume. It contains some of the finest oils to be found in plants. May I suggest then, that the problem is not the soybean; the problem rather is the way it has been grown and prepared.

The first genetically modified soybeans were planted in the United States in 1996, today genetically modified herbicide resistance plants are widespread with over 90 percent of U.S. corn, cotton, and soybeans produced using GE varieties.[1] Currently no GM crops are being grown commercially in the UK although scientists are carrying out controlled trials. When GM soy is eaten, it can cause major problems especially when it is not organically grown and is refined so that the isolate of the bean is used for food. Allergies to soy only began appearing after it had been genetically modified.[2]

In 2022 the United States introduced new national labeling standards for food that's been genetically modified, labeling them as "bioengineered" or "derived from bioengineering," however establishments like restaurants don't have to comply with the new rule. Likewise, biotechnology companies aren't required to report which genetically modified seeds are used in production.[3] Genetically engineered crops and can be found as an ingredient in a wide range of foods such as chocolate, potato chips, margarine, mayonnaise, cookies and bread. In fact, soybean oil accounts for 61% of Americans' vegetable-oil consumption.

Considering the issues we have just discussed, it is essential that the soy products you buy are made from soybeans that have not been genetically modified, have been organically grown and the whole soybean used. The easiest way to eat the soybean is as tofu, which is very easy to digest and very high in protein. Remember that tofu is a tasteless sponge but is very quickly turned into a gourmet delight with the appropriate flavourings.

Chapter Nine References

1 "Economic Research Service, U.S. Department of Agriculture," *Recent Trends in GE Adoption* (2022), <www.ers.usda.gov/data-products/adoption-of-genetically-engineered-crops-in-the-u-s/recent-trends-in-ge-adoption/>, accessed August 2023.

2 The Institute for Responsible Technology <https://responsibletechnology.org/genetically-engineered-foods-may-cause-rising-food-allergies-part-one/>, accessed March, 2020.

3 *Time Magazine* <https://time.com/3840073/gmo-food-charts/>, accesed March 2020.

—CHAPTER TEN—

Acid and Alkaline Balance

Precision is everything

Fungus thrives in an acid environment.

Acid and alkaline environments are expressed on a scale of pH. The pH stands for 'potential hydrogen.' When acid dissociates into water it gives off hydrogen ions, so when testing how acid a solution is, you are actually testing how many hydrogen ions are in the solution. When alkaline dissociates into water, it gives off hydroxyl ions. Neutral indicates equal hydrogen ions and equal hydroxyl ions; thus, it is neither acid nor alkaline but neutral. Even slight deviations above or below the norm can signal potentially serious and dangerous states of imbalance.

The pH scale is like a thermometer showing increases and decreases in the acid and alkaline content of body fluids. Just as a correct pH balance is vital in the swimming pool and for the hydroponic gardener, so it is in the human body. If the water in the swimming pool becomes acidic, the pipes corrode; if it becomes too alkaline, algae grow on the pipes.

The pH balance is the regulatory authority that controls most cellular processes.

Our body pH controls the speed of our body's biochemical reactions. It does this by controlling the speed of enzymatic activity as well as the speed that electricity moves through our body. Therefore, electricity travels slower with a higher pH. An easy way to remember is if something has an acid pH, it is like saying it is hot and fast. Alkaline pH is slow and cool.

The blood pH is constantly being balanced by the lungs and the kidneys. Slight variations have a dramatic effect on the body's biochemical reactions as already noted. At a blood pH of 7.22, the organism goes into a coma and dies of acidosis. At a blood pH of 8, the organism goes into a coma and can die of alkalosis. Although the blood pH is kept at a constant balance, the cellular pH can change. This can be tested by litmus paper in the urine and saliva.

The most acidic substance is sulphuric acid. On a scale of speed, it travels at the speed of light. The most alkaline mineral is calcium. On a scale of speed, it doesn't even move. The lungs and the kidneys are constantly monitoring the acid-alkaline balance but in extreme and constant acidic conditions, the body reverts to pulling calcium phosphates out of the bones in a last resort effort to alkalise the acid condition.

This process explains why many people today suffer from weak bones, or osteoporosis.

FUNGUS RELATIONSHIP TO ACID

When bacteria, yeasts and fungus are active in the human body because of cell damage or a massive infiltration, their wastes create a very acidic condition. Not only do these microforms create an acidic condition in the body but they also thrive and readily multiply in an acidic environment. Maintaining a correct pH in the body is an important part of preventing these organisms multiplying and thus an essential component in eliminating fungus and cancer.

This explains why Dr. Tullio Simoncini is experiencing such success with sodium bicarbonate. Sodium bicarbonate is highly alkaline. Its presence is found in the lining of the stomach, to neutralise any acid that might penetrate the mucus lining. The pancreas is another organ that naturally produces sodium bicarbonate. The release happens in response to the acidic state of the food leaving the stomach and entering the duodenum. In both cases the sodium bicarbonate is used primarily as an alkaliser.

As Dr. Simoncini found, the sodium bicarbonate alkalises whatever it touches. This poses a problem to the inaccessible areas in the body; for instance, the liver, the brain, the pancreas and the kidneys. The answer to this dilemma lies in a very simple and easily accessible food that is highly alkaline. Green foods!

THE GREAT ALKALISERS

Green vegetables and grasses are an excellent source of the alkaline salts that are antifungal. The greener the better! The green juice extracted from plants is not only one of the most alkalising foods there is, but it is also a potent tissue and blood cleanser.

Chlorophyll is the pigment constituent that makes plants green. The structure of the chlorophyll molecule is almost identical to our own blood molecules. As a result, chlorophyll can build haemoglobin in blood. Some of the impressive therapeutic benefits of chlorophyll include:

1) It is rich in the antioxidant SOD (superoxide dismutase), which has the ability to clear radiation, chemicals, pollutants and other toxins from our cells.
2) Limits the growth of many types of viruses and harmful bacteria.
3) Stimulates repair of damaged cells.
4) Protects against the damaging effect of toxic chemicals and radiation.
5) Deodorises and cleanses tissues, thus reducing offensive body and breath odors.

Green-up your intake of food by eating a big green salad every day. Make it sparky with one of the exciting salad dressings included in the recipe section. Salads love to be dressed! Another way to green-up your intake is to include a green supplement into your diet every day such as green barley or wheat grass juice. Green-up your intake with green drinks.

These green drinks are the most potent way to cleanse and alkalise the tissues in the body. Second best is to take a powder green supplement, like green barley, wheat grass or spirulina. If you live in the country, you cannot improve on the Great Green Drink (see page 85). But for the city dwellers, the powdered greens are an attainable alternative.

Recipe for the Great Green Drink

- **4 cups of wild crafted greens***
- **4 cups of pure water**

1. Place in blender, and blend until the plants are broken up and the fluid is green. This may need to be done in a few batches, maybe two or three blenderfuls. It will depend on the size of your blender.
2. Strain through a fine sieve. Pour into four small glass bottles and screw the lid on, then refrigerate. This is a daily dose.
3. Take one bottle four times a day, preferably between meals. Don't keep for more than twelve hours.
4. To drink, remove the lid and take a mouthful. Keep the fluid in the mouth for ten seconds before you swallow, all the while making sure you move the vital green fluid around in your mouth to ensure the enzymes in your mouth are well mixed with the potent nutrients, oils and other plant chemicals this elixir of life contains. Keeping the lid on between mouthfuls reduces the loss of volatile oils.

* Wild crafted refers to plants that grow wild by continually self-seeding to reproduce themselves, in comparison to hybrid plants who are incapable of reproducing. Being deficient in this essential mechanism has an effect on the eater at a cellular level. When a plant has lost its ability to reproduce, it has lost a specific nutrient required in the cell to run the energy cycle.

Wild crafted greens refers to anything green that is edible, even grass! Let me help you—dandelion, chickweed, dock, all mints, stinging nettle, purslane, parsley, celery leaves, turnip leaves, carrot tops, beet tops, lettuce, fresh coriander, basil, lemon grass. Basically if it's green and edible, throw it in! One easy way is to watch what the cows, goats and sheep eat.

An important point to remember is to alternate your greens. The body gets used to the same things and alternation keeps the body reactive.

FOODS THAT AFFECT THE pH BALANCE

Inside the cells of our body is a little furnace, called the mitochondria. This is where our food, which has been broken down to a single molecular structure of glucose, is burnt to produce energy. What's left of the food is an ash, a chemical and metallic residue that combines with our body fluids to form a pH of either acid or alkaline. Certain foods leave an acid ash, while others leave an alkaline ash. It depends mostly on the mineral composition of the food.

The Acid – Alkaline Graph

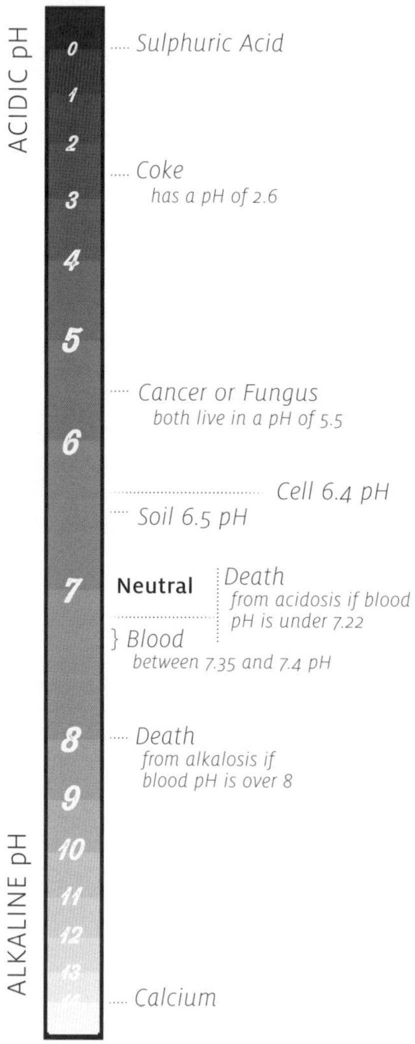

Alkaline-forming elements include: Calcium, potassium, magnesium, sodium, even iron.

Acid-forming elements include: Sulphur, phosphorus, chlorine and iodine.

On the next page is a basic breakdown of acid- and alkaline-forming foods—that is, foods that leave an acid ash or alkaline ash when burnt in the cell.

This chart begins with the most acid-forming foods down to the most alkaline-forming foods.

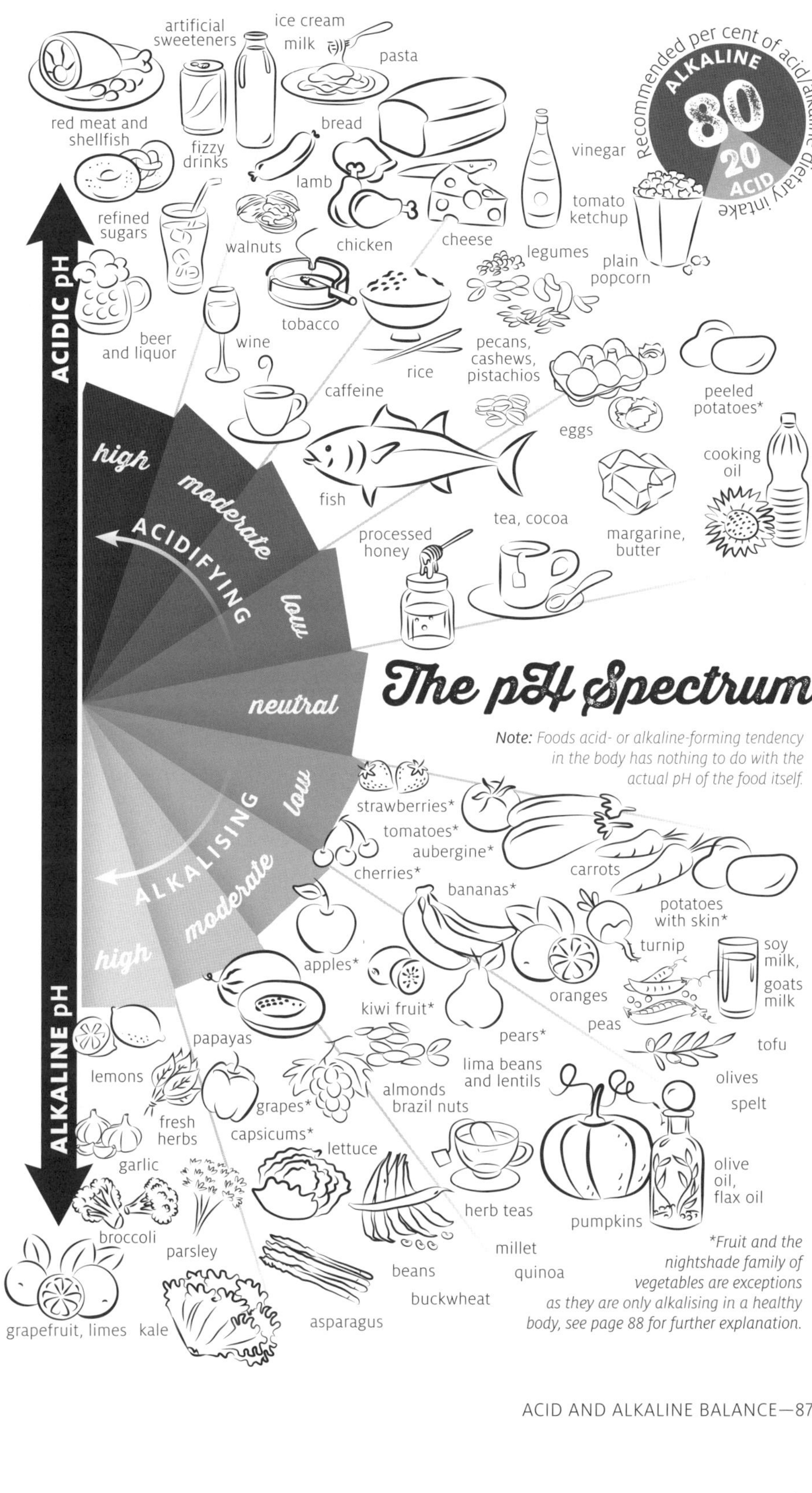

The pH Spectrum

Note: *Foods acid- or alkaline-forming tendency in the body has nothing to do with the actual pH of the food itself.*

**Fruit and the nightshade family of vegetables are exceptions as they are only alkalising in a healthy body, see page 88 for further explanation.*

THE EXCEPTIONS

Fruit

When fruit is taken into a body that has a yeast/fungus problem, the sugar in the fruit is snapped up fast by the fungus. Fungus loves sugar. It prefers refined cane sugar, but it will happily accept the glucose in the fruit. The resulting waste the fungus leaves is lactic acid, acetic acid, uric acid and alcohol. This acid waste creates the very environment where fungus can quickly multiply. In a body with no fungus problem, fruit can be alkalising and cleansing.

Example: A 38-year-old lady contacted me for help with a skin rash, which had appeared on her chin. Her husband had seen his eczema on his legs and arms totally clear up in the last few months by following the program outlined in this book. As fungus can travel through body fluids, I was not surprised at this lady's rash. But fungus will only grow if the environment is right.

Upon investigation it was revealed that two recent occurrences had triggered the growth of the fungus that had manifested itself on the chin. First was the return of her periods after an 18-month break while breast feeding her baby. This caused the release of more oestrogen, which is a growth stimulant. This alone could not have done it, but in conjunction with a huge meal of fresh figs (about 20) the scales were tipped. The excess sugar entering the body from the generous amount of figs enabled the fungus to receive the necessary sugar for its multiplication. In this lady's case, the fungus manifested itself on her chin.

The nightshade family of vegetables

Tomatoes, aubergine (eggplant), capsicums (sweet peppers) and potatoes are from the nightshade family. When an inflammatory condition is active in the body, for example arthritis, this group of vegetables has an effect to increase inflammation. An exception is when the tomato is cooked without the skin. When the skinned tomato is cooked with olive oil over a slow heat, it releases a potent antioxidant called lycopene. Lycopene inhibits inflammation, especially of the prostate gland.

If the body is not in an inflammatory condition, then these vegetables tend to an alkaline effect. Of the nightshades, in a human without inflammation, the tomato is the most alkaline. Each person needs to fine tune the application for themselves.

RECOMMENDATIONS

It is recommended that a person's food program contain 80 percent alkaline-forming foods and 20 percent acid-forming foods. This proportion will aid the body in maintaining a correct pH balance of 6.5 in the cell. Slightly acid is necessary to maintain the electrical speed in the cell.

The easiest way to maintain the correct pH balance in the body is to eliminate cane and beet sugar in all its forms, alcohol, all caffeine drinks and foods and tobacco. Ideally, meat and dairy products are best avoided or greatly reduced, while increasing the consumption of vegetables and other alkaline-forming foods.

LIFESTYLE PRINCIPLES THAT AFFECT THE ACID/ALKALINE BALANCE

These life style principles can be remembered in a simple acronym "Sustain Me". Making a habit of these lifestyle principles can sustain you, and so you help others to be sustained and enjoy a longer happier and healthier life.

PRINCIPLE 1: Sunshine

"I think you might dispense with half your doctors, if you would only consult Dr Sun."—Henry Ward Beecher

Too much sunshine and too little sunshine can cause an acidic condition in the body. Human bodies need sunshine as much as the plants. Only an hour a day helps alkalise the body. A good guide as to when it's safe to be in the sun is when your shadow is as long as you are.

The sun's rays hitting the skin converts a form of cholesterol just under the skin to vitamin D. Vitamin D in its active form has the ability to inhibit cancer cell growth. Vitamin D is essential in the assimilation and metabolism of calcium in the body. Vitamin D is needed to take the calcium into the cell.

Only ten minutes on the face a day will give you all the vitamin D you need. There are seven times more blood vessels on the face. The body is very efficient at storing vitamin D, and can store it for up to six months. As not all days are sunny, more than 15 minutes a day is recommended.

Sunshine is a potent fungus killer and can protect the body from cancer. Allow the cleansing, healing sunshine to touch your body and enter your homes. It will purify the air and everything it touches.

Your eyes need sunshine. Never should we look directly at the sun. Being outside allows the sun's rays to enter the retina and travel through neurochemical pathways to hit the pineal gland, which helps you sleep better at night and increases the release of serotonin, your mood hormone. This is why you feel happier on a sunny day.

A word of caution if your body is not used to the sun: begin with short frequent bouts, and as your body takes on a slight tan, you will find that you can comfortably stay in the sun a little longer.

PRINCIPLE 2: Use of Water

"Water is the basis of life, and the blue arteries of the earth." —Sandra Postel

Water alkalises. Many people experience an acidic condition in their body because of dehydration. Approximately two to three liters of water is lost from the average-sized human body every day. We have no reserve tank on the back, the only water that goes in is the water we put in. Two to three liters of pure water must be taken into the body every day to replace this loss. An increase in physical activity and very hot days may demand more.

Water is best taken between meals. Cease half an hour before the meal, and resume two hours after the meal. This allows the digestion to perform its work unhindered. It is very important to be well hydrated when beginning to dine. Water drunk with meals dilutes hydrochloric acid, which the body needs to be able to digest protein.

The cells of the body are able to accept the water more easily when the water is taken little by little throughout the whole day. When water intake is increased, sodium loss can increase and so it is essential to ensure adequate salt intake as well. The magnesium contained in the Celtic salt increases the delivery of water into the cell.

PRINCIPLE 3: Sleep

"Early to bed and early to rise makes a man healthy, wealthy, and wise."

"Sleep is the golden chain that binds health and our bodies together."
—Thomas Dekker

Too much sleep and too little sleep can both create an acidic condition in the body.

Remember the old saying "an hour before midnight is worth two after midnight"? Allow science to explain this wise counsel.

There is a small gland in the base of your brain called the pineal gland. Light and dark signals are fed through the optic nerve to a control centre in the brain where the body clock is located. The body clock communicates with the pineal gland. This gland releases four hormones between the hours of 9 pm and 2 am.

- **Serotonin**—this is the mood hormone. The more serotonin you have, the happier you will feel.
- **Epithalamin**—increases learning capacity and slows down ageing.
- **Arginine Vasotocin**—has an effect on sleep and pain. This is the hormone that puts you into a deep sleep and is also your built-in painkiller.
- **Melatonin**—responsible for rest and rejuvenation.

The cells of the body regenerate at twice the rate when sleeping. Early nights ensure this promised restoration and this is the sleep that alkalises the body.

The pineal gland receives clear signals when the eyes experience sunrise, sunshine, sunset and the dark night. If you are having trouble sleeping, you can reset your body clock by putting your alarm clock on so that you wake just before sunrise. Experience the setting sun too!

The cells of the body regenerate at twice the rate when sleeping. Early nights ensure this promised restoration and this is the sleep that alkalises the body.

The Bible states, 'the sleep of a labouring man is sweet.' The physical exhaustion created by physical exercise induces a deep, sweet sleep.

There is one organ of the body that is dependent upon periods of rest, but that luxury is rarely allowed it—the stomach!

Humans have one stomach that takes three to four hours to digest a meal. After this, the stomach likes an hours rest. This rest-time is used to replace and replenish digestive enzymes in preparation for the next meal.

The stomach also likes to sleep when the rest of the body sleeps. For this request to be granted, the evening meal needs to be the lightest meal of the day. To be able to achieve this, breakfast and lunch need to be more substantial.

As the old saying goes, "Eat breakfast like a king, lunch like a queen, and tea like a pauper."

Or reckon breakfast like gold, lunch like silver, and tea like lead!

Considering all this, it is highly recommended that approximately five hours be left between meals. With the inclusion of fibre, protein and healthy fats at the first two meals, this time frame is easily accomplished, especially when water is drunk between meals.

PRINCIPLE 4: Trust in Divine Power (Mental Health).

Stress creates an acid environment in the body. Laughter is one of the best pressure releases from stress

"Against the assault of laughter, nothing can stand."—Mark Twain

"A merry heart doeth good like a medicine:
but a broken spirit dries up the bones."—Proverbs 17:22

Laughing creates a merry heart and science tells us that healing hormones are released when we laugh.

The previous lifestyle habits mentioned create a nutritionally stable and strong physical body. This gives a foundation that effectively empowers a person to deal with stress.

A positive attitude, a merry heart and trust in Divine Power can all do much to contribute to peace in the soul. The Bible says, "Thou wilt keep him in perfect peace, he whose mind is stayed on Thee, because he trusteth in Thee" (Isaiah 26:3). That soothing picture spells alkaline.

Faith is the alkaline emotion, while fear is the acid emotion.

Grief, anxiety, discontent , remorse, guilt, resentment, distrust, all tend to break down the life forces and invite decay and death into the body. This alarming picture spells acid.

Our emotions affect us physically; fear and its associated emotions can compound and even create disease, while faith with its accompanied emotions can heal. Faith is an inseparable companion of hope. "Faith is the substance of things hoped for, the evidence of things not seen" (Hebrews 11:1).

Hope sees the invisible; feels the intangible; and achieves the impossible.

"God has not given us the spirit of fear, but of power, love and of a sound mind"—2 Timothy 1:7.

In the last decade, science has discovered that the brain can be rewired. This means that even the most negative and fearful person can become positive and of great faith! To do this we need to be diligent in ensuring that the most positive and uplifting information is planted in the garden of our minds. Make sure no weeds get in!

Our emotions affect us physically; fear and its associated emotions can compound and even create disease.

PRINCIPLE 5: Abstain

"Our own physical body possesses a wisdom which we who inhabit the body lack. We give it orders which make no sense."—Henry Miller

One of the crazy habits people often have is the taking into the body of poisonous substances that are mistakenly viewed as safe.

Alcohol, caffeine in all its forms, refined sugar, tobacco, drugs, chemicals, heavy metals and even too much good food cause an acidic condition in the body. Eliminating this list from the diet is essential in maintaining the body's correct pH balance.

Alcohol: A neurotoxin, or brain poison. Nerve cells are all through the human body with the greatest concentration being in the brain and spinal cord. When alcohol is taken, it directly inhibits the healing powers of the body. It is extremely acidic and fungus loves it.

Caffeine: One of the most alarming things about this highly toxic, highly addictive drug is its availability. This lulls a person into thinking that it is safe. Nothing could be further from the truth. The lift it gives is a delusion as it comes with a guaranteed drop. This is one of the reasons it is so addictive.

Another reason is caffeine's effectiveness in disrupting brain chemistry by the dropping and rising of different neurotransmitters (chemical messengers). Due to the disruption of the neurotransmitters in the brain, the nerve cells attempt to compensate in an effort to try and maintain the precision balance that proper brain function requires. This explains the terrible headaches that are experienced when the caffeine is stopped. Caffeine creates an extremely acidic condition in the body.

Sugar: The refining of sugar cane produces an extremely dangerous, highly acidic substance called sucrose or sugar. This toxic acid is a highly addictive drug. The truth of this is witnessed when the drug is withdrawn. It not only is the single most responsible substance for fungal growth, but it also creates the highly acidic environment that fungus loves. Eating this stuff is like rolling out the red carpet and saying to fungus, "Come right on in!"

Tobacco: The presence of gases produced by smoking cigarettes is one of the most powerful ways to inhibit oxygen availability in the cell. This deprivation of oxygen to the cell is an open invitation to fungal development, whether you are the smoker or whether you are a passive smoker. This and the 4000 chemicals contained in the cigarette all contribute to a very acidic condition in the body.

Drugs: The body does not know the difference between legal and illegal drugs. All create an acidic condition.

"COFFEE MUST MAKE YOU SLEEPY.
THEY'RE ALWAYS SLEEPY WHEN THEY DRINK IT."

Chemicals: Never in the history of mankind have human beings been subject to so many chemicals. The body stores many of these toxic substances in our fat cells. Everyone can do something to reduce their contact with chemicals as they all have an acidic effect on the body. Some simple tips—eat organically grown food and use only biologically safe cleaning products for house, clothes and body.

PRINCIPLE 6: Inhale (fresh air),

"Air, air, the precious boon of heaven, which all may have, will bless you with its invigorating influence, if you will not refuse its entrance."—Ellen White

Air contains oxygen. Oxygen is the most vital element needed for life on planet earth. The lungs inhale oxygen and exhale carbon dioxide (the gas waste from the cell).

Oxygen alkalises, carbon dioxide acidifies, and the correct balance of these two gases is vital to allowing oxygen into the cell. Inhaling and exhaling through the nose will insure the balance.

Oxygen vitalises, invigorates and electrifies the body, as well as soothes the nerves.

Oxygen is the essential component of aerobic cells. If oxygen is unavailable to the cell, it must resort to using the process of fermentation to produce energy. This is an anaerobic cell. Less oxygen means less aerobic cells and more anaerobic cells. Fungal cells and cancer cells are both anaerobic cells. This explains why cancer cannot grow in the presence of oxygen.

To increase the oxygen content of the cell:

- Correct breathing habits are vital. Breathing through the nose and with the abdominal muscles greatly increases the uptake of oxygen in the human body. Nose purifies, warms, humidifies, pressurises and modulates the blood gasses. Mouth does not do this.
- Good posture is essential to allow the abdominal muscles, which were designed to aid in the breathing process, full expansion.
- Exercise **is** the most effective way to increase oxygen uptake into the body. More exercise equals more oxygen.
- Breathe fresh untainted air.

Air contains oxygen in the form of negative and positive ions.
Negative ions are electrically charged oxygen molecules and are found:

- in a thunderstorm
- by the sea with crashing waves
- at the waterfall
- in the forest; the leaves of plants purify the air.

Positive ions contain more carbon dioxide in their molecule than oxygen.
These are found:

- before a thunderstorm
- in pollution, smog and car fumes
- in rooms that are heated with a naked flame, such as gas and combustion fires
- in strong wind
- in mould waste.

Many people with yeast and fungus problems, including cancer, complain of no energy and chronic fatigue. All fungus cells function anaerobically, that is without oxygen. An aerobic cell, that is a cell that runs on oxygen, gives 18 times more energy compared to an anaerobic cell. This explains the lack of energy.

PRINCIPLE 7: Nutrition

There are foods that create an acid environment in the cell.

There are foods that create an alkalised environment in the cell.

A correct balance of these foods create a healing environment, which this chapter has just explored.

PRINCIPLE 8: Moderation

The body runs according to precision balance, a correct acid/alkaline balance is required to maintain balance.

Salt is vital and is often over or under done.

"Salt is born of the purest of parents: the sun and the sea." —Pythagoras 580BC

Sodium is the third most vital element needed for life. Sodium should be taken into the body the way it is found in nature. The largest concentration of sodium is found in sea water. Sea water contains 92 minerals.

Celtic and Himalayan salt are both unrefined sea salts that contain approximately 82 minerals. The table salt or common salt that is found on the supermarket shelf contains only two minerals—sodium and chloride. This is a harsh salt and a dangerous salt because it causes an electrolyte imbalance by bringing sodium into the body in an unbalanced way. If sodium chloride were to be injected into the body, the person would die.

The human body requires sodium in a balanced state, the way it is found in nature, accompanied by a host of other minerals. When sodium is taken in this form it has an alkalising effect in the body, and ensures a proper mineral balance. You see, our tears are salty, our blood is salty, our urine is salty, and the baby in utero swims in salt water.

The unrefined salts quoted contain three magnesiums—magnesium chloride, magnesium sulphate and magnesium bromide. These three magnesiums go on patrol around the body tissues looking for excess sodium to eliminate.

Refined salt, which contains two minerals, sodium and chloride, has a very acidic effect on the body.

"Ye are the salt of the earth: but if the salt have lost his savour, wherewith shall it be salted? it is thenceforth good for nothing, but to be cast out, and to be trodden under foot of men."—Matthew 5:13

Refined salt has lost its "*savour*", or minerals, this has converted a alkalising salt into an acid salt.

PRINCIPLE 9: Exercise

"More people rust out than wear out."—Bishop Richard Cumberland

Too much exercise and too little exercise can both create an acidic condition in the body.

Stagnant pools breed disease and stagnant bodies breed disease.

Strength comes through exercise, and activity is the very condition of life.

Exercise is the most effective way to increase oxygen availability to every cell in the body and oxygen alkalises.

Cancer cannot live in the presence of oxygen.

The body runs according to precision balance, and balance must be maintained by equal brain and body activities.

Self healing is possible when it is understood that God designed the living machinery to be in activity daily; in that activity is its preserving power.

For exercise to be a preservative it must contain certain components. Rebounding, is an exercise usually performed on a device known as a rebounder—sometimes called a "mini-trampoline", is the only exercise that combines, defying gravity, acceleration and deceleration as well as this, it is very gentle. There is no jarring to the joints and spine. Every cell in the body is effected, the circulatory and lymphatic systems are stimulated.

High Intensity Interval Training (H.I.I.T.) combines intervals of high intensity and recovery. This can effectively be done on the Rebounder. Beginning with the health bounce and working up to jumping and jogging for high intensity, then back to the simple health bounce.

The high intensity exercise causes a release of the Human Growth Hormone. (HGH), which:

- Increases the body's ability to utilise protein
- Stops burning glucose as fuel and instead burns fat as fuel
- Releases an enzyme in the cell which triggers the release of adipose fat stores
- Increases the circulation of the blood to the skin.

It is the release of the HGH that athletes rely on to give them a power boost in their physical feats. Understanding the effect this hormone has on the body explains why exercise gives such a healing boost. Part of this is the alkalising effect.

The best exercises are Rebounding, cycling and swimming as they can incorporate the H.I.I.T. And yet there is no damaging jolting to joints.

Not only the heart, lungs, bones and muscles are strengthened by exercise, but the internal organs are also toned and strengthened to perform their work.

Perfect health requires,perfect circulation. Exercise, and exercise alone stimulates the circulation of the blood and lymphatic fluids.

Discover more about these simple health principles and how they can help cure disease in my new book *Sustain Me*.[1]

1 *Sustain Me: A Hand Book on Natural Remedies*. by Barbara O'Neill, Due for release early 2024.

—CHAPTER ELEVEN—

The Stomach's Secret Weapon

Hydrochloric acid and digestion

"Sweet to the mouth, bitter to the stomach; bitter to the mouth, sweet to the stomach."—Anonymous

One of the most powerful weapons of our self-healing body is Hydrochloric acid (HCl). Hydrochloric acid is an enzyme that is made in the liver and released into the stomach when food is introduced into the mouth. It is an essential component when conquering yeast and fungus problems in the body as HCl is a potent fungicide. When HCl levels are at optimum levels, a portion is absorbed into the bloodstream. The entrance of HCl into the blood spells death to blood-borne fungus.

Current research reveals that after the age of 20, most people lose 10 percent of their digestive enzymes per decade.

Our food needs to literally swim in the enzyme pool in the stomach—ideally 3200mg to 4000mg of HCl per meal.

Most people suffer from so-called 'acid stomach' (reflux and indigestion) because of low amounts of HCl. This causes the food to linger in the stomach too long in an insufficiently digested state, which in turn results in the food beginning to ferment. It is this fermentation that produces the acid condition, and the accompanying bloating.

The liver is the organ that is responsible for the production of the main digestive enzyme—hydrochloric acid. To do this, the liver requires two cups of water, the day before, per meal. Two cups of water on Tuesday, for Wednesday's breakfast, and another two cups Tuesday for Wednesday's lunch, and so on. Thus dehydration is a big contributing factor to digestive impairment. The water required by the liver to produce Wednesday's HCl must be drunk on Tuesday, approximately two cups per meal.

The liver has a measuring stick for the amount of HCl to be produced per meal. The measuring stick for lunch is given by the amount of HCl that was released for breakfast.

Hydrochloric acid functions include:

- Converting pepsinogen to pepsin, which is the proteolytic enzyme that breaks down protein
- Opening interior bonds of the protein structure to aid access from pepsin
- Releasing various nutrients from organic compounds (food)
- Acting as a bactericide and fungicide agent that kills bacteria and fungi that may come in with food.

In the ideal environment of 3200mg to 4000mg of HCl per meal, residues of this powerful enzyme can be absorbed into the blood and aid in the destruction of yeast and fungus in the blood.

Gastrin is a gastrointestinal hormone that:

- Stimulates the release of hydrochloric acid (HCl) and other digestive enzymes
- Causes cell growth in the stomach wall
- Increases gastric motility (movement).

Gastrin is released by the G cells in the stomach. This release occurs in response to:

- Different foods entering the stomach
- Distension of the stomach
- Partially digested protein reaching the lower part of the stomach
- HCl coming in contact with the mucosal lining of the stomach.

How to aid in the production of hydrochloric acid

Following are some tips that aid in the production and maintenance of sufficient amounts of HCl.

1. **Drink 2 liters water daily between meals.** Stop 30 minutes before meals and resume two hours later. Taking water with meals dilutes HCl, which in turn inhibits its digestive and antibacterial/fungicidal activity. Dehydration inhibits the release of gastrin at meal times. Dehydration prevents the liver from producing adequate HCl. The body should be well-hydrated when you sit to eat.
2. **Drink lemon juice.** Lemon just before or with meals increases HCl activity.
3. **Include protein in the first few mouthfuls of food consumed at a meal.** When partially digested protein reaches the lower part of the stomach it initiates the release of more gastrin.
4. **Chew the food slowly and thoroughly.** This allows the food to be broken into smaller particles, allowing a larger surface area for the digestive enzymes to work on. Thorough chewing gives specific messages to the brain allowing it to convey to the appropriate organs the type of foods that are on their way. Thus the correct amount and type of enzymes are prepared and waiting to digest the food as it comes down the digestive tract.
5. **Stop eating.** To increase gastrin release at meal times, stimulation must be prevented between meals. An average meal takes three to four hours to digest. After this mighty effort the stomach deserves a well-earned rest. Thus five hours is needed between meals to allow for digestion and a short rest. This will ensure full recovery and storage of the digestive enzymes. Unwanted stimulation includes eating between meals and chewing gum. Coffee and alcohol also stimulate gastrin release; this is why they are known to contribute to stomach ulcers.

6. **Eat or drink bitter herbs.** There are a few herbs and foods that specifically stimulate the release of HCl. These bitter herbs include:

   - Cayenne Pepper
   - Dandelion
   - Fennel
   - Garlic
   - Gentian
   - Ginger
   - Golden Seal
   - Green Drinks
   - St. Mary's Thistle

7. **Don't worry.** Stress and anxiety at meal times inhibits gastrin release. The atmosphere at the dining table must be relaxed and cheerful.
8. **Drink some warm water.** One-third of a cup of very hot water just before eating brings the blood quickly to the stomach, which increases gastrin release.
9. **Get some Betaine Hydrochloride.** Betaine Hydrochloride is an enzyme extracted from beets that can be a powerful tool in bringing the HCl in the stomach up to its full amount.

In some cases proteolytic enzymes may need to be used. Proteolytic enzymes are released in the stomach specifically for protein digestion. HCl is released in the stomach; it connects with pepsinogin to release pepsin. Pepsin is a proteolytic enzyme. The pancreas releases trypsin and chymotrypsin, which are also proteolytic enzymes. Vegetarian sources of proteolytic enzymes are papain from the pawpaw, and bromelain from pineapple.

—CHAPTER TWELVE—

Liver

The Project Manager

"If the manager smiles, the whole work place smiles."

The liver is the body's project manager and master chemist. As such it is essential to have it working at optimum efficiency in the quest for maintaining wellbeing, or for conquering disease.

This organ is extremely busy, as is evidenced by its huge blood flow. Every 14 minutes, all your blood passes through your liver.

Everything that enters the body goes straight to your liver. The liver is the largest internal organ in the body. A unique feature of the liver is its ability to heal itself and regenerate cells, especially when supported nutritionally. It is the only organ in the body with this ability.

As the project manager, the liver determines what is to be done with every entry. Cancer cannot get a hold on the body while the liver is working efficiently.

To understand how to support the liver in its role in the body, let us consider its functions, and in so doing, understand its needs.

THE LIVER'S FUNCTIONS

1. The liver manufactures bile salts that are stored in the gall bladder and released in the small intestine for the emulsification and absorption of fats.
2. The liver, together with the mast cells, manufactures the anticoagulant heparin, and also most of the other plasma proteins such as prothrombin, fibrinogen and albumin.
3. The liver stores glycogen, copper, iron, and vitamins A, D, E and K. It also stores some poisons that cannot be broken down and excreted.
4. The liver determines the future of everything we eat. Food is broken down to an absorbable state (glucose) in the gastrointestinal tract, absorbed through the villi that line the intestines, and lands on the main highway (the portal vein) that takes it straight to the liver. The liver sends a portion of the glucose to the cell to be burnt as fuel. A small amount is stored in quick-release packages, called glycogen. Glycogen is stored in the liver and muscle cells. The remaining glucose is sent to the storage areas in the body, called fat. The liver can call on these stores when needed, for example, blood glucose levels falling, flight or fight situations, and convert them back to glucose. If carbohydrate levels are low, the liver has the ability to manufacture glucose from fat or protein.
5. The liver detoxifies excess oestrogen. As oestrogen is broken down in the liver it can be taken down two main pathways—the 2-hydroxy pathway or the 16-hydroxy pathway.

   If oestrogen is taken down the 16-pathway, it is recirculated back into the body 100 times more toxic. But if the 2-pathway is taken, it is excreted out of the body. Vitamin B6, B9 and B12, liquorice herb and the cabbage family all encourage the 2-pathway while they discourage the 16-pathway.
6. If anything enters the body that is toxic, the liver has the ability to alter the structure to make it less toxic and easier to excrete. But some substances that are extremely toxic are wrapped up in fat and stored, until the body is in a state of optimum nutritional status and the tools are available to facilitate its alteration and removal.

Most toxins come in the form of drugs, alcohol, chemicals, hormones, pesticides, heavy metals, tobacco and so on. The majority of these chemicals that enter the body are in a fat soluble state, and this is why they are stored in the fatty tissues. It is difficult to eliminate toxins in a fat soluble state. The overall goal of the liver is to take these fat soluble, toxic substances and make them more water soluble and non-toxic, through a series of chemical reactions. It can then be easily excreted via the skin, sweat glands and bowels.

The liver accomplishes this very important task in three phases.

> The overall goal of the liver is to take these fat soluble, toxic substances and make them more water soluble and non-toxic,

PHASE ONE

In phase one, fat soluble toxins are broken down to a metabolite. This metabolite is a result of the first stage of metabolism or breakdown of toxins. It is a highly reactive stage, creating a lot of free radicals, and in some cases producing a substance which is 100 times more toxic than it originally was.

To cope with this volatile and potentially damaging stage the liver requires:

A) **Antioxidants**—Antioxidants are called free radical scavengers because of their ability to give extra electrons to free radicals, thus stabilising them. Antioxidants are essential at this stage to provide protection, reduce tissue damage and reduce unpleasant symptoms. The most potent antioxidant is beta carotene. This is found predominantly in yellow and green coloured vegetables. Vitamin C (ascorbic acid) comes in close behind. Make sure your ascorbic acid is accompanied by bioflavonoids. Vitamin E rates third in the most potent antioxidants. Being a fat soluble vitamin it is found in seeds, nuts and legumes—particularly soy.

   Glutathione is a powerful antioxidant. It assists in the detoxification of heavy metals, as well as protecting cells. Carrots and cabbages are high sources of this non-essential amino acid. This explains why carrot juice is such a good tonic, for it is high in not only glutathione, but also beta carotenes.

B) **B vitamin complex**—Required for energy to push the detoxification process and for the specific pathways. These vitamins are not stored and so must be replenished daily.

C) **Minerals**—Magnesium, zinc, molybdenum, copper, selenium and potassium.

D) Herbs—Specifically herbs that stimulate liver function, such as Saint Mary's Thistle and dandelion.

E) Fatty acids—Omega 3 and 6 provide cell membrane protection.

PHASE TWO

Phase two involves conjugating, or joining, the metabolite with amino acids, which creates the water soluble state that enables it to be safely excreted.

The liver now needs:

1. Sulphur-bearing amino acids such as cysteine and taurine. Vegetarian proteins adequately supply these amino acids. The legume family of pulses contains the highest amount. The addition of garlic and onion increases the sulphur when cooking legumes.
2. Brassica family of vegetables, these include cabbage, broccoli, brussels sprouts, kale and cauliflower.
3. Turmeric
4. St. Mary's Thistle, a powerful antioxidant, at least ten times stronger than vitamin E and can increase the glutathione levels in the liver by 35 percent.

The phytonutrients in the last three points stimulate the phase two enzymes to work at a higher level.

Balancing is essential

Ideally phase two should match phase one, so that the toxic metabolites produced are processed quickly and safely. The best way to achieve a balanced liver detox is to minimise the amount of reactive metabolites by gently reducing phase one and *enhancing* phase two.

PHASE ONE REDUCERS	PHASE ONE INDUCERS. *These substances must be avoided as they increase Phase one activity.*	PHASE TWO ENHANCERS *These substances are needed to keep the balance between the different phases.*
Turmeric	Alcohol	Brassica
Grapefruit	Caffeine	Turmeric
Garlic	Nicotine	St. Mary's Thistle
Echinacea	Stress	B6, B12
Watercress		Folate
		Protein-rich foods such as legumes and nuts*

* The seed of a plant contains all the elements needed to produce life. Legumes, grains, nuts and seeds are the seeds of plants and so provide an excellent pool of the essential amino acids needed for the liver's requirements.

PHASE THREE

This stage is called the anti-porter system, or two-way system. Here the liver eliminates the water soluble state as it pulls in any more toxins that need the structural alteration rendering them safe via the three phases of liver detox. The main need of the liver here is the essential fatty acids omega 3 and 6, which effectively give fluidity yet integrity to the cells involved. Flaxseed is the highest source, with chia seed not far behind. Walnuts, sunflower seed, olives and almonds contain a small amount and added to the daily program can help lift fatty acid levels.

During a fasting program where water or juices are taken, one of the main nutrients withdrawn is protein. This leads to a reduction in amino acids, thus resulting in diminished phase two activity. Now phase two is unable to keep up with phase one activity, which means there are highly toxic, potentially damaging metabolites (reactive intermediates) accumulating! The corresponding symptoms of nausea, headaches, diarrhoea are usually interpreted as a 'healing crisis', while the truth is that it is a liver crisis! Behind the scenes the liver is actually catabolising its own tissue in an attempt to provide the amino acids needed to create the safe, water soluble state.

How to Maintain a Happy Liver

VEGETABLES: Include generous amounts of vegetables in your daily food program, and some fruits.

SUNSHINE: Allow the sun to penetrate the skin to the liver. Lay in the sun with discretion, often.

LAUGH: "A merry heart doeth good like a medicine." The liver is no exception!

BITTER HERBS: The liver loves bitter herbs such as dandelion, St. Mary's Thistle or gentian.

PROTEIN: Have protein every meal. Vegetarian options such as legumes, nuts and seeds are superior.

HEALTHY FATS: Such as olive oil, all forms of coconut, seeds and nuts—these need to be part of every meal as they keep the liver's bile production alive and vibrant.

B VITAMINS: A regular supply of the full range of B vitamins.

SLEEP: Bed by 9pm, to allow the liver to revive, rest and recharge.

LEMON: A lemon a day is an effective liver tonic.

BE REGULAR: Keep the colon regular. Daily evacuations are essential. The toxic fumes given off from a sluggish colon put an unnecessary load on the liver.

EXERCISE: One ½ hour exercise a day at least. Brisk walking is best as it tones and strengthens the liver.

ERADICATE POISONS: Keep the poisons (alcohol, drugs, chemicals, heavy metals, tobacco and refined sugar) out! Regular high doses of fructose are a liver toxin. As the liver is the only organ with fructose receptor sites, high doses force the liver to store it as fat. Hence, fatty liver. High dose fructose is found in fruit juice, sugar-free jams and various health bars. Especially dangerous are cakes and biscuits containing high fructose corn syrup. Fruit will not do this as the fructose is in its natural state.

WATER: Drink at least two liters of water a day, between meals. The liver requires two cups of water the day before, to produce enough HCl for one meal.

LIVER CLEANSE

Give the liver a kick-start with a liver cleanse.

This will take five days. If the body is quite ill, this may need to be repeated several times, over several months—in some cases a week on and a week off.

Liver Cleanse

- ½ cup fresh orange and lemon juice
- ½ cup of pure water
- 1 clove of garlic*
- 1 tablespoon of olive oil*
- ½ a teaspoon of chopped ginger (this will negate any nausea).

1. Blend all ingredients
2. Drink upon rising on an empty stomach.

*This is the dose on day one. Day two double the garlic and the oil. Day three triple it. Day four is as day two and day five is as day one.

Fifteen minutes after this, cleanse your system by drinking one glass of hot *liver tea.*

Liver Tea

- 1 part dried dandelion root
- 1 part dried St. Mary's thistle
- 1 part dried gentian
- 1 part dried liquorice
- ½ part dried golden seal
- 1 part fresh ginger when cooking

1. Put one teaspoon of the dried herbs, with one teaspoon of the fresh ginger, into two cups of water. Gently simmer with the lid on for fifteen minutes.

The week that this program is taken, the bowels must be cleansed every day by taking approximately one cup of *Colon Tea* each night. (The amount will differ depending on the needs/health of the colon.) Ideally there should be at least two bowel evacuations per day.

Colon Tea

- 1 part cascara segrada*
- 2 parts liquorice
- 3 parts buckthorn

1. Take one teaspoon of this tea mix to one cup of water. Gently simmer for fifteen minutes with the lid on. Consume one cup of the tea before going to bed.

* Cascara sagrada is a natural herbal laxative made from the reddish-brown bark of a tree (Rhamnus purshiana). It contains compounds called anthroquinones, which trigger contractions in the colon, causing the urge to have a bowel movement. Cascara sagrada can be found in various forms such as capsules, liquid extracts, and dried bark, which, when made into tea, can taste very bitter.

When this program is being considered to eliminate gallstones, a *Castor Oil Compress* needs to be applied to the liver area for at least five hours a day.

Castor Oil Compress

- Towelling
- Castor Oil
- Plastic wrap

1. Moisten two layers of towelling with castor oil. Cover with plastic to prevent the oil spoiling clothes. Make sure the whole liver area is well covered.

Castor oil penetrates deeper than any other oil and has the ability to break up lumps, bumps and adhesions. As part of this program it can soften and break down the gallstones as well as lubricating the bile duct, thus aiding in the expulsion of the gravel/stones.

This compress should be worn around the liver area for at least five hours every day. Ideally this should be done for the week before and during the liver cleanse.

GO ASK CAESAR WHAT HE WANTS IN HIS SALAD.

—CHAPTER THIRTEEN—

Recipes

Meals to promote health and healing

Welcome to an important section of the book that will help you to make legumes the most exciting dish at your table.

Comments on Legumes

A common complaint with legumes is the wind factor. Most people do not rinse their legumes enough. It will be noted when cooking legumes that a white froth often forms on top. This is what creates the wind and it must be rinsed away. Some legumes require more rinsing than others. The state of the water is the best indication of the need to rinse. Soaking the legumes also aids in the digestion process. The larger legumes usually require more soaking than the smaller legumes. On the next page are guidelines as to how to prepare them for cooking.

Cooking Legumes guide

When cooking dried beans and legumes, soak overnight and rinse well before cooking. To cook, add enough water to cover the beans with a two inches of water, bring the beans to the boil, then rinse again, and bring to the boil a second time with fresh water. When half way through the cooking time, rinse once more and at this point you can add seasoning or other ingredients as required.

LEGUME	SOAKING TIMES	APPROXIMATE COOKING TIME
Lima Beans	Soak overnight, and prepare as guided above.	2–3 hours
Small Lima Beans	Soak overnight, and prepare as guided above.	1–1 ½ hours
Red Kidney Beans	Soak overnight, and prepare as guided above.	2 ½–3 hours
Cranberry Beans (Borlotti Beans)	Soak overnight, and prepare as guided above.	1 ½–2 hours
Chickpeas (Garbanzo Beans)	Soak overnight, and prepare as guided above.	2–3 hours
White Beans (Cannellini/ Great Northern Beans)	Soak overnight, and prepare as guided above.	1 ½–2 hours
Black Turtle Beans	Soak overnight, and prepare as guided above.	2–3 hours
Soybeans	Soak for 24 hours, and prepare as guided above.	3 hours

LEGUME	SOAKING TIMES	APPROXIMATE COOKING TIME
Green and Yellow Split Peas	Soak overnight, and prepare as guided above.	45–60 minutes
Green (brown) Lentils	Soak overnight, and prepare as guided above.	30–45 minutes
Black-eyed Peas	These beans cook very quickly compared to other beans their size and so can be cooked without soaking. They must be rinsed at least three times while cooking.	1 hour
Chana Dahl and Moong Dahl	Wash dahl very well, soak them for 30 minutes before cooking. Add 2 ½ cups of water for every 1 cup of dahl	½–1 hours
Red Lentils	No need to soak but must be rinsed until the water is clear, bring to the boil in fresh water, immediately rinse, and cover with fresh water, add any seasoning then simmer for 10 minutes. If overcooked, they have the consistency of mashed potato.	

The above is an approximate guide as there can be quite a variation depending on the freshness and the size of the legumes.

Tinned legumes can be used—there is quite a variety of organic legumes now available in tins and they can be a very convenient alternative when time is a factor.

To make legume cooking easier, it is a good idea to soak several varieties overnight, rinse in the morning, strain and store in 1–2 cup portions in bags in the freezer.

Breakfast Suggestions

Quick Green or Brown Lentils — *Serves 4*

Ingredients:

1 cup green or brown lentils

½ cup water

1 tsp Celtic salt

1 Tbsp olive oil

1 tsp Italian herbs

1 large tsp miso

Method:

1. Cover the lentils well with water and bring to the boil. Rinse twice then bring to boil again. Turn heat down to low and simmer with the lid on for approximately 25 to 30 minutes until soft.
2. When soft, strain the lentils and add salt, olive oil, herbs and miso, mixing very well. Heat through and serve on toast.

Scrambled Tofu — *Serves 4*

Ingredients:

1 block firm tofu

1 tsp grated garlic

1 tsp grated ginger

2 tsp Celtic salt

1 ½ tsp turmeric

1 tsp Italian herbs

¼ cup chopped fresh parsley

2 Tbsp water

2 Tbsp olive oil

Method:

1. Crumble tofu and add the rest of the ingredients. Cook over medium heat for 10 minutes.
2. A nice dish served on toast with tomatoes and avocado.

Scrambled Tofu

Simple Black-eyed Peas — *Serves 4*

Ingredients:

1 ½ cup black-eyed peas, soaked overnight

2 crushed cloves garlic

½ tsp finely chopped ginger

1 tsp miso dissolved in water

1 tsp Italian herbs

1 tsp Celtic salt

1 Tbsp olive oil

Method:

1. Rinse peas several times, then bring to boil. Change water, and bring to boil again. Simmer gently for 50 to 60 minutes, until soft.
2. Add garlic, ginger, miso, herbs, olive oil and salt.
3. Serve on toast with avocado for breakfast, or with salad and rice for a main meal.

Quick Red Lentils — *Serves 6*

Ingredients:

2 cups red lentils, rinsed 4 times

2 tsp Celtic salt

2 tsp turmeric

2 tsp basil or Italian herbs

4 Tbsp olive oil

Method:

1. Bring the red lentils to boil but don't let them boil, drain and rinse again.
2. Put lentils back in the saucepan, add the salt, turmeric, herbs and olive oil, then enough fresh water just cover the lentils.
3. Place a lid on the lentils and bring to boil again, then simmer gently for 5 to 10 minutes until the lentils are soft.
4. Lovely served on toast.

Main Meal Suggestions

***Note:** the following recipes contain the instructions 'gently sauté onions'. To explain this: the onions are put into a dry pan over a low heat with the lid on. The condensation dripping from the lid and the juice contained in the onion will be enough moisture for the onion to brown nicely, but the heat must be low or the onion will burn. The oil is added later with moisture as this prevents the oil going to too high a temperature and destroying the essential fatty acids contained in the oil.

Tasty Lima Beans — *Serves 4*

Lima beans are also known as butter beans. They are a member of the kidney bean family. When cooked, these beans have a soft texture that blends well into creamy style dishes. A nice addition to this recipe is to mix in 1 cup of steamed asparagus at the end.

Ingredients:

1 ½ cups lima beans, soaked overnight
½ cup cashews
1 clove garlic
1 heaped tsp Celtic salt
½ tsp Italian herbs
1 cup water
Chopped fresh parsley

Method:

1. Rinse the lima beans several times before cooking. When almost cooked, rinse and add fresh water then bring back to the boil till soft; strain off water then blend till smooth (approx. 2–3 hours, total cooking time).
2. To make cashew sauce, combine cashews, garlic, salt, water and herbs in a blender until smooth.
3. Combine cashew sauce with lima beans and parsley and heat through.

Chickpea Cardamon Casserole — *Serves 6–8*

Chickpeas are believed to be one of the earliest cultivated legumes originating in the Middle East. They are also known as garbanzo beans, shimbra or ceci beans.

Ingredients:

1 medium onion
2 cloves garlic
2 cm (¾ inch) piece finely chopped ginger
3 cups cooked chickpeas (garbanzo beans)
1 tsp cardamon seeds
4 skinned chopped tomatoes
1 Tbsp tomato paste
2 tsp Celtic salt
½ cup finely chopped celery
½ cup finely chopped carrot
⅓ cup olive oil

Method:

1. Sauté onions on a low heat until clear and slightly golden. Add ginger and garlic and cook another 5 minutes.
2. Add tomatoes, celery, carrots, olive oil and cardamon seeds. Gently simmer for 30 minutes.
3. Add chickpeas, Celtic salt and tomato paste (add a little water if too thick), and gently simmer for another 20 minutes.

Red Kidney Beans—*Mexican Style — Serves 6–8*

Kidney beans generally take between 3 and 4 hours to cook. Do not add any salty seasonings until after the beans have been cooked. Adding them earlier will make the beans tough and greatly increase the cooking time. Rinse after cooking.

Ingredients:

4 cups cooked red kidney beans
2 cups chopped onion
2 ½ cups chopped tomatoes
1 cup finely chopped celery
1 cup finely chopped carrot
2 cups diced tofu
1 tsp cumin
2 tsp Celtic salt
1 tsp turmeric
2 cloves fresh garlic
½ cup olive oil

Method:

1. Sauté onion on a low heat until slightly golden and then add garlic and cook a further 5 minutes.
2. Add tomatoes, olive oil, celery and carrot. Gently simmer for 30 minutes.
3. Add kidney beans, tofu, turmeric, cumin and salt. Simmer for another 30 minutes.

Chickpeas with Spinach — *Serves 4*

The cartoon character Popeye the Sailor Man is portrayed as becoming physically stronger after consuming Spinach. While this may be quite an over-exaggeration spinach does have a high nutritional value and is extremely rich in antioxidants. Leafy green vegetables such as spinach provide more minerals than any other food, making it quite the superfood. This dish goes beautifully served with the Noodle Salad (page 144).

Ingredients:

1 cup cooked chickpeas (garbanzo beans)
1 onion finely sliced
2 cloves garlic
1 tsp fresh ginger
6 cups finely chopped spinach
2 Tbsp olive oil
1 tsp Celtic salt

Method:

1. Lightly sauté onion over a low heat until lightly golden. Add garlic, ginger and spinach. Allow the spinach to wilt over a low heat with the lid on.
2. Add chickpeas and olive oil and salt. Cover and allow to gently cook enabling the flavours to blend.

Creamy Beans and Cauliflower — *Serves 4*

To help make the sauce creamy soak the cashews for a minimum of two hours, or preferably overnight, before blending.

Ingredients:

- 1 ½ cups soaked, rinsed and cooked white beans (cannelloni beans or great northern beans)
- 1 finely sliced onion
- 1 cup raw cashews
- 2 cloves garlic
- 2 cups water
- 1 tsp celtic salt
- 1 Tbsp olive oil
- 1 cubed carrot
- 2 cups small cauliflowerets *or* 1 cup broccoli and 1 cup cauliflower
- 2 tsp fresh marjoram (or 1 tsp dried marjoram)

Method:

1. Lightly sauté onion until lightly golden over a low heat. Place carrots on onions and cook on a low heat for 5 minutes.
2. Meanwhile, blend cashews, water, garlic and salt until smooth and pour into onions and carrots. Add cauliflower (broccoli) and beans. Simmer over a low heat with lid on until cauliflower is just tender.
3. Add olive oil and fresh marjoram. Simmer a few more minutes and serve. (Add a little water if too thick.)

Pumpkin and White Bean Curry — *Serves 4–5*

There are many different types of pumpkin (squash) you can get, and each variety has its own unique flavour, with some taking longer to cook than others.

Ingredients:

1 kg (2 lb) chopped butternut squash or kabocha (pumpkin)
1 Tbsp olive oil
1 Tbsp water
1 medium chopped onion
2 cloves crushed garlic
1 tsp grated ginger
300 g (10.5 oz) cooked or raw chopped asparagus
400 g (14 oz) white beans (precooked)
½ cup coconut milk
55 g (2 oz) baby spinach leaves
1 Tbsp fresh finely chopped basil
2 tsp Celtic salt

Dried spices:

½ tsp ground coriander
½ tsp fennel
½ tsp fenugreek
½ tsp cumin
½ tsp turmeric

Method:

1. Sauté onion over a low heat in own juice until clear. Add garlic and ginger, chopped pumpkin and olive oil and water. Cook for another 10 minutes with the lid on over low heat.
2. When the pumpkin is almost cooked, add asparagus, white beans and the dried spices. Cook for another 10 minutes with lid on (add a little water if needed).
3. Add the coconut milk, spinach, basil and salt. Stir gently until hot.

Indian Curry — *Serves 6*

This can be served on freshly cooked brown rice with a green salad, or for added protein and fibre served with cooked quinoa instead of rice.

Sauce:

3 onions
1 cup olive oil
2 tsp fresh coriander
1 tsp cumin
1 tsp turmeric
1 tsp paprika

Ingredients:

2 chopped potatoes
2 chopped carrots
1 cup chopped butternut squash (pumpkin)
1 cup chopped broccoli
1 cup chopped cauliflower
1 cup peas or beans
2 cups soaked, rinsed and cooked white beans (cannelloni beans or great northern beans)
2 tsp Celtic salt

Method:

1. To make sauce, blend onions, with enough water to allow blending, until liquefied. Pour into saucepan and cook until starting to bubble. Add olive oil, place lid on and cook over a very low heat for 15 minutes.
2. Add herbs to the sauce and cook for another 15 minutes.
3. Add potatoes, carrots and pumpkin and cook on a low heat for 1 hour.
4. Add the remaining ingredients and cook for a further 15 minutes. Add 2 teaspoons of Celtic salt and a little water if the curry is too thick.

Coconut Kaffir Lime Tofu — *Serves 6–8*

Kaffir lime leaves are the fragrant leaves of the wild lime tree found in South East Asian countries and are used widely in their local cuisine. You can purchase the leaves from either Asian food stores or the Asian section in some supermarkets.

Ingredients:

1–2 whole kaffir lime leaves
1 medium chopped onion
2 tsp grated ginger
1 tsp turmeric
2–3 cloves crushed garlic
400 g (14 oz) block chopped firm tofu
400ml (1 tin) Thai coconut milk
2 chopped carrots
1 cup chopped broccoli
1 cup chopped cauliflower
2 tsp of Celtic Salt

Method:

1. Sauté onion on a low heat until lightly golden. Add ginger and garlic and lightly cook another 5 minutes. Add tofu and turmeric and kaffir lime leaves. Place lid on and allow to cook for 15 minutes over a very low heat to prevent sticking, add a little water if necessary.
2. Add coconut milk and salt. Warm through but do not bring to boil. Take pot off the stove and let sit for at least 1–2 hours.
3. Lightly steam vegetables 10 minutes before serving. Gently stir through tofu mix. Bring almost to the boil and serve.
4. Nice served with rice and a green salad.

Pesto Beans — *Serves 6–8*

Basil, being high in chlorophyll, helps balance acid within the body and restore the body's proper pH level. This can also improve digestion and immunity by helping healthy bacteria flourish within the gut microflora, while also decreasing harmful bacteria that can cause disease.

Ingredients:

2 cups basil leaves
½ cup olive oil
2 cloves garlic
¾ cup cashews
¼ cup sunflower seeds
2 tsp Celtic salt
⅓ cup lemon juice
1 cup water
4 cups cooked white beans (such as cannelloni, great northern or small lima beans).

Method:

1. Blend garlic, cashews, sunflower seeds, salt, water and lemon juice until smooth. Add basil leaves and olive oil. Blend until smooth.
2. Fold pesto through 4 cups hot cooked white beans. Serve with salad, baked vegetables and Lebanese green beans. This dish can be served hot or cold.

Eastern Vegetable Curry — *Serves 6*

This curry is nice served on freshly cooked brown rice cooked with turmeric.

Ingredients:

- ¾ cup chickpeas (soaked)
- 1 medium thinly sliced onion
- ¾ cup red lentils
- 1 small aubergine (eggplant), cut into 2 cm (½") cubes
- 1 cup butternut squash (pumpkin) cut into 2 cm (½") cubes
- 2 large skinned tomatoes cut into 2 cm (½") cubes
- 1 ½ cups baby spinach leaves
- ½ cup olive oil
- ⅓ cup flaked almonds
- 2 tsp Celtic salt

Dry Spice Mix:

- 2 tsp turmeric
- ½ tsp cardamom seeds
- 1 ¼ tsp coriander
- ¼ tsp fenugreek seeds
- ⅛ tsp cayenne pepper (optional)

Curry Paste:

- 2 large cloves finely grated fresh garlic
- 1 Tbsp finely grated fresh ginger
- 1 cup fresh coriander
- 1 cup fresh mint
- 6 Tbsp water

Method:

1. Rinse and cook the chickpeas until almost soft, rinse and set aside.
2. Rinse the lentils several times and bring to the boil but don't let them boil. Drain, rinse and set aside ready for combining with the other ingredients.
3. Preheat oven to 180ºC (400ºF). Brush the cut pumpkin with a little oil and place on a tray in the oven. Bake until golden brown.
4. Sauté onions* on a low heat until almost clear, and then add the dry spice mix. Cook for 3 minutes.
5. Add tomatoes and aubergine and cook on low heat for 20 minutes.
6. To make the curry paste, combine garlic, ginger, coriander, mint and water.
7. Now add the curry paste to the cooked and drained lentils, chickpeas and the oil and salt. Allow this mixture to gently simmer for approximately 10 minutes. Gently fold through the baked pumpkin and spinach leaves.
8. Heat through well and serve on brown rice cooked with turmeric (optional), topped with flaked almonds.

* *See note on page 119*

Eastern Vegetable Curry

Matthew's Savoury Lentils

— Serves 6

This is my son-in-law's speciality and is delicious served with baked vegetables, steamed greens and salad.

Ingredients:

2 cups soaked, rinsed and cooked green or brown lentils
1 medium chopped onion
2 cloves crushed garlic
1 tsp grated ginger
2 chopped skinned tomatoes
1 cup finely sliced celery (with leaves)
1 cup finely chopped carrot
2 Tbsp olive oil
2 tsp basil
1 tsp oregano
2 tsp paprika
½ cup crumbled tofu
2 tsp Celtic salt
1 Tbsp tomato paste
2 tsp dark miso, mixed to a paste in a little water

Method:

1. Lightly sauté onion until lightly golden. Add ginger and garlic. Sauté another 5 minutes.
2. Add tomatoes, celery, carrots, flavourings and olive oil and cook over a low heat for another 10 minutes. Add cooked lentils and crumbled tofu and allow this to simmer for another 15 minutes.
3. Add salt and tomato paste (and a little water if too thick) and cook for another 5 minutes. Add miso, mix well and serve.

Lebanese Green Beans — *Serves 6*

Ingredients:

1 large onion
3 skinned chopped tomatoes
2 Tbsp olive oil
4 cups sliced green beans
1 heaped tsp Celtic salt

Method:

1. Sauté the sliced onion on a low heat until slightly golden. Add tomatoes and cook for 5– 10 minutes. Add olive oil and mix well.
2. Add beans, replace lid and allow this mixture to cook over a very low heat for about 15 minutes until beans are almost soft.
3. Add salt, mix well and allow to cook for a few more minutes.

Lovely Lima Beans — *Serves 6*

Lima Beans, also known as Butter Beans, have a distinctive buttery texture and sweet flavour. They are an important source of plant proteins and have more potassium than red kidney beans, broad beans or black beans. This dish is nice served with baked vegetables, steamed greens and a salad.

Ingredients:

2 cups cooked lima beans (see page 114)
1 large finely sliced onion
2 cloves crushed garlic
2 cups finely sliced celery (with leaves)
4 skinned, finely chopped tomatoes
⅓ cup olive oil
2 tsp Celtic salt
1 tsp basil

Method:

1. Gently sauté onion until golden. Add garlic, celery, tomatoes, basil and olive oil. Simmer with lid on over a low heat for 15 minutes.
2. Add lima beans and salt; mix well, return lid and gently simmer another 5 minutes.

Barbara's Black Beans — *Serves 6*

Serve with either brown or basmati rice, and a fresh green salad.

Ingredients:

2 cups cooked black turtle beans (see page 114)
1 finely sliced large onion
2 cloves crushed garlic
2 tsp finely grated ginger
4 large peeled and chopped tomatoes
¼ cup olive oil
2 sticks finely sliced celery (with leaves)
1 large finely diced carrot
1 Tbsp tomato paste
1 Tbsp freshly chopped basil
2 tsp freshly chopped oregano
½ tsp maple syrup
2 tsp Celtic salt

Method:

1. Lightly sauté onion over a low heat until slightly golden. Add garlic, ginger, tomatoes, celery, carrot and olive oil and very gently simmer over a very low heat, covered, until carrots are tender (approximately ½ hour).
2. Add beans, herbs, tomato paste, salt and maple syrup. (Add a little water if too thick.)
3. Gently stir and lightly simmer for a further 5 minutes.

Barbara's Black Beans

Split Pea Dahl — *Serves 4*

Dahl is a major part of Indian cuisine. It is said no Indian meal is ever complete without a bowl of dahl. There are infinite ways of cooking dahl, here and on the following page are a few of my personal favourites. Best served with brown or basmati rice and Indian flat bread, accompanied by a tossed salad. Be careful not to overcook.

Ingredients:

1 ½ cups cooked green split peas (see page 114)
2 tsp finely grated ginger
2 tsp finely grated garlic
1 large finely chopped onion
½ tsp turmeric
1 tsp cumin
2 tsp dried coriander
1 Tbsp fresh coriander
2 tsp Celtic salt
⅓ cup olive oil

Method:

1. Cover split peas well with water and simmer for 45 minutes. Rinse well. These will be partially cooked.
2. Sauté onion until lightly brown. Add ginger and garlic and continue to sauté another 5 minutes with lid on. Add turmeric, cumin and dried coriander and olive oil. Lightly simmer on a very low heat another 5 minutes.
3. Add the partially cooked split peas and one cup of water. Gently simmer on a low heat until peas are soft. If the Dahl becomes too dry, add a little more water. The consistency of the Dahl should not be too runny, nor too thick, but almost like a sauce. Add salt.
4. Stir in fresh coriander just before serving.

Lentil and Spinach Dahl — *Serves 4*

Like the Split Pea Dahl, this dish can be served with rice, Roti (Indian flat bread), bowls of sliced tomato, cucumber and soy yoghurt, and shredded lettuce. If you like your Dahl hot, cayenne pepper can be added to taste just before serving.

Ingredients:

- 1 ½ cups cooked brown or green lentils (see page 114)
- 2 tsp finely grated garlic
- 2 tsp finely grated fresh ginger
- 1 finely chopped onion
- 1 bunch chopped spinach
- 1 tsp turmeric
- 1 tsp cumin
- 2 tsp dried coriander
- 2 tsp Celtic salt
- ⅓ cup olive oil

Method:

1. Sauté onion until lightly brown. Add garlic and ginger and continue to lightly sauté with lid on for a further 5 minutes.
2. Add cumin, turmeric, coriander, oil and spinach. Simmer another 5 minutes with lid on until spinach is lightly wilted.
3. Add lentils. Mix well, return lid and allow to lightly simmer for approximately 5 minutes. Add salt and allow to simmer just a few more minutes for the salt to disperse.

Sunshine Dahl — *Serves 6*

Moong Dahl are light yellow mung beans that have been skinned and split, so that they're quick-cooking. They are rich in protein and a staple food in India. Serve the Dahl with rice and roti for a healthy wholesome meal.

Ingredients:

2 cups soaked moong Dahl (or yellow split lentil)
1 large chopped onion
2 cloves crushed garlic
2 tsp finely grated ginger
1 large diced carrot
2 cups cubed butternut squash (pumpkin)
2 skinned, finely chopped tomatoes
2 cups chopped celery leaves
⅓ cup olive oil
2 tsp ground coriander
1 tsp cumin
1 tsp turmeric
2 tsp Celtic salt

Method:

1. Rinse the lentils several times and bring to the boil, and simmer for five minutes. Drain, rinse and set aside ready for combining with the other ingredients.
2. Lightly sauté the onion over a low heat until lightly golden. Add garlic, ginger, tomatoes and the three spices. With the lid on allow to lightly simmer for 10 minutes.
3. Add pumpkin, carrot, olive oil and lightly simmer another 10 minutes.
4. Add moong Dahl, celery leaves and enough water to cover the ingredients by about half an inch. Return lid and allow to gently simmer, stirring often, for approximately 15 minutes until the dahl is soft. Add salt and more water if too thick.

Soups

Split Pea Soup — *Serves 4*

A bowl of this soup delivers a bounty of nutritional benefits—a good amount of vegetable protein and plenty of staying power. Delicious served with a green salad and hot crusty sourdough bread.

Ingredients:

2 cups cooked green split peas (see page 114)
1 large chopped onion
2 chopped carrots
1 cup sliced celery
1 cup chopped celery leaves
1 cup chopped butternut squash (pumpkin)
2 tsp Celtic salt
⅓ cup olive oil
½ cup chopped fresh green mint

Method:

1. Lightly sauté onion over a low heat until lightly golden.
2. Add carrots, celery and leaves, pumpkin, and peas and cover with water. Bring to the boil, turn to a low heat and allow to gently simmer for at least 1 hour.
3. Add water if necessary to attain desired consistency. Add salt, oil and mint. Simmer for just a few minutes to allow the flavourings to disperse throughout the soup.

The Mighty Minestrone Soup — *Serves 6–8*

Never underestimate the power of a humble bowl of vegetable soup. Full of nutrients, this easy minestrone soup packs loads of vitamins and minerals into every spoonful.

Ingredients:

2 cups borlotti, cranberry beans or red kidney beans, soaked, rinsed, brought to the boil and rinsed again (see page 114)

1 finely diced onion

2 cloves crushed garlic

1 finely diced carrot

2 cups finely sliced celery (with leaves)

2 cups tomatoes, skinned and sliced

2 finely chopped potatoes

1 cup finely chopped butternut squash (pumpkin)

1 cup chopped broccoli

1 cup chopped cauliflower

⅓ cup olive oil

2 tsp Celtic salt

2 bay leaves

1 tsp marjoram

1 tsp thyme

1 tsp rosemary

2 Tbsp tomato paste

Method:

1. Lightly sauté onion over a low heat until tender. Add carrots, garlic, celery, tomatoes, potatoes, pumpkin, olive oil and bay leaves and lightly simmer over a low heat for 10 minutes.
2. Add prepared beans to vegetables and cover with water. Allow to gently simmer for 1 ½ – 2 hours until beans are soft.
3. Add broccoli and cauliflower, salt, remaining herbs, tomato paste and more water if too thick. Let simmer another 10 minutes and serve.

Lentil Soup — *Serves 6*

Lentils are nutritious and taste great in soups. On bone-chilling winter days, nothing says comfort like a steaming bowl of warm soup. This is a delicious winter meal served with garlic sour dough bread and a large fresh salad.

Ingredients:

2 cups green or brown lentils (rinsed)
4 cloves garlic
1 chopped onion
2 cubed carrots
3 cubed potatoes
2 sticks celery (with leaves)
2 tsp marjoram
2 tsp paprika
1 tsp thyme
2 bay leaves
2 tsp miso
2 tsp Celtic salt
2 tbsn olive oil
water

Method:

1. Lightly brown onion and garlic in a saucepan, add the other vegetables, cover with water and simmer until soft.
2. Rinse the lentils, cover with a few inches of water and then bring to boil and simmer for 20 minutes until almost cooked, rinse them and set aside.
3. To the pot of vegetables, add the lentils, bay leaves and half the amount of herbs and enough water to cover all ingredients. Bring to the boil and simmer for 20 to 25 minutes.
4. Add remaining herbs, salt, miso and olive oil. Mix thoroughly and simmer a few minutes more, then serve. If a thinner soup is desired, add more water.

Lentil Soup

Salads

Noodle Salad — *Serves 4*

Ingredients:

200 g (7 oz) dried pasta noodles
2 Tbsp olive oil
Juice of 1 lemon
½ tsp finely grated lemon rind
2 tsp Celtic salt
1 clove crushed garlic
½ cup sliced black olives
½ cup sliced sun-dried tomatoes
1 tsp Italian herbs
½ cup fresh parsley

Method:

1. Cook pasta as per directions on the packet in well-salted water.
2. Rinse pasta well and toss with oil and all other ingredients.
3. This dish can be served hot or cold.

Greek Salad — *Serves 6–8*

Greek salads traditionally feature feta cheese. Tofu is a tasteless sponge and this marinade brings it to life. Marinated tofu makes a delicious alternative to feta cheese.

Tofu Marinade:

- 1 tsp grated ginger
- 1 tsp crushed garlic
- 1 tsp Celtic salt
- 1 tsp miso
- ¼ cup lemon juice
- ¼ cup olive oil
- ½ tsp maple syrup
- 1 tsp basil
- 1 tsp paprika
- ½ tsp oregano

Salad Ingredients:

- 400g (one pack) firm tofu cut into 2 cm (½") cubes
- 3 fresh coarsely chopped tomatoes
- 1 coarsely chopped Lebanese or English cucumber
- 1 small thickly chopped red onion
- ½ cup chopped celery
- 1 chopped courgette (zucchini)
- ½ cup black olives

Method:

1. Mix the marinade ingredients together well and pour over the tofu leaving to marinate for at least 1 hour.
2. Add the tomato, cucumber, onion, celery, olives and courgette (zucchini).
3. Mix well and serve.

Lentil Salad — *Serves 4*

Lentils can range in colour from green, khaki-brown or dark black. They are high in protein, iron and fibre, making them a healthy staple for vegetarian diets. They cook in about 45 minutes by boiling and hold their shape very well.

Ingredients:

- 1 cup cooked green or brown lentils (see page 114)
- 1 chopped onion
- 4 chopped tomatoes
- 1 chopped courgette (zucchini)
- ½ cup chopped fresh parsley
- ½ cup chopped fresh coriander
- 2 tsp finely grated ginger
- 1 tsp finely grated lemon rind
- 1 small chopped capsicum (optional)

Dressing:

- ⅓ cup lemon juice
- ½ cup olive oil
- 2 tsp Celtic salt

Method:

1. Mix all the salad ingredients together.
2. Thoroughly shake the dressing ingredients in a jar.
3. Pour dressing over the salad and toss to combine.

Lentil Salad

Red Kidney Bean Pâté

Pâté and Dips

Red Kidney Bean Pâté

If you're wondering how to replace red meat in your menus, become a fan of kidney beans. These hearty beans are a good source of protein. This recipe is extremely easy to make and tastes great. Serve with tortilla chips, crackers or vegetable sticks.

Ingredients:

1 cup cooked red kidney beans (see page 114)
2 tsp Celtic salt
½ tsp paprika
½ tsp cumin
1 clove crushed garlic
Juice of 1 lemon
2 tsp olive oil
2 tsp tahini
1 Tbsp water (enough to get desired consistency of a soft cream)
½ cup finely chopped fresh parsley

Method:

1. Either blend everything in a food processor (you might need to add a little extra water if it's a bit sticky), or mash beans in a bowl with a potato masher, then stir in everything else.

Houmous

Houmous is a traditional Middle Eastern chickpea spread and a major part in the diet of many healthy populations living around the world. When the ingredients in houmous are combined, they offer many health benefits. This has to do with the way that the fats, carbohydrates, and proteins found in houmous work together to give us a feeling of satiety after eating it.

Ingredients:

- 1 cup cooked chickpeas
- 2 Tbsp tahini*
- Juice of 2 lemons
- ½ tsp finely grated lemon rind
- 2 tsp Celtic salt
- 2 cloves crushed garlic
- 1 cup water
- 1 Tbsp olive oil

Method:

1. Blend ingredients in a blender until smooth, or mash together well with a fork.

** Tahini is made of ground sesame seeds. It can be used as a sandwich spread, or mixed with a variety of other seasonings such as garlic and onion or cayenne pepper for a tasty dip or salad dressing.*

Houmous

Sunflower Seed Pâté

Sunflower seeds are an incredible source of health-benefiting nutrients, minerals, antioxidants and vitamins. They also contain Omega 3 and Omega 6 and are very high in protein.

Ingredients:

1 ½ cups sunflower seeds
½ cup lemon juice
½ tsp salt
1 clove garlic
½ tsp light or white miso dissolved in ¼ cup water

Method:

1. Soak sunflower seeds 36–48 hours, making sure the seeds are sprouted. (When they start sprouting, they will look like the open beak of a bird.)
2. Place all the ingredients in a food processor and blend until smooth. Keeps for 5 days in fridge.

Salad Dressings

Tahini Mayo Dressing

Ingredients:

2 Tbsp lemon juice
1 tsp Celtic salt
½ cup water
1 clove garlic
¼ cup tahini
¼ tsp maple syrup
2 Tbsp olive oil

Method:

1. Blend all ingredients together and chill. Add more water if too thick.

Tahini Dressing

Ingredients:

½ cup cashews
3 Tbsp olive oil
3 Tbsp lemon juice
¼ tsp maple syrup
1 cup water
3 large cloves garlic
1 Tbsp tahini
Celtic salt to taste

Method:

1. Place all ingredients in blender, and blend until smooth. Keeps for 5 days in fridge.

Garlic Linseed Dream

Linseed, also known as flaxseed, is a rich source of omega 3 essential fatty acids. Because it comes from a plant source, it is perfect for vegetarian and vegan diets, although it benefits everybody.

Ingredients:

1 Tbsp linseed/flaxseed, soaked in 1 cup of water overnight
10 cloves garlic
½ tsp Celtic salt
½ tsp maple syrup
½ cup lemon juice
1 tsp basil
½ tsp oregano
½ tsp marjoram
½ cup olive oil

Method:

1. Blend linseed/flaxseed, garlic, Celtic salt, maple syrup and lemon juice in a blender until smooth.
2. Add herbs and oil and blend on low for a few seconds. Parsley can be added to hide the strong garlic flavour. Keeps for 5 days in fridge.

Index

Pictured: *Barbara (far right) and her six children, December 2013.*

About the Author—Barbara O'Neill

Barbara O'Neill was born in 1953 in Ingleburn, New South Wales, Australia. Barbara was born into a conventional Australian home and she was the second child with one older brother and three younger sisters. Her father owned and operated a Shell Service Station at Lugarno, NSW, and Barbara had the misfortune to see her mother die at the young age of 51 from rheumatoid arthritis.

Barbara's first work on leaving school was as a hairdresser and some years later trained and worked as a psychiatric nurse at North Ryde Psychiatric Hospital.

Barbara's journey into natural health commenced when her first child Emma contracted whooping cough and spent 6 weeks in hospital. This became the motivation for Barbara to search out the cause, find a remedy and live a lifestyle that would prevent this from happening again.

With her partner, she embraced an alternative 'hippie' lifestyle and moved from Sydney to a north NSW rainforest area west of Coffs Harbour.

Removed from close proximity to conventional medical facilities Barbara studied health and home schooled her six children. Her reputation grew as a 'healer' and people brought their sick children to her for advice and assistance, and she became locally known as 'earth mother'.

In addition to her passion for health, Barbara embraced Christianity at 26 years of age. This put her on a new path to look at the human body in the light that it is not a product of random uncontrolled evolution, but that it was intricately designed with all its in-built mechanisms to self-heal. Barbara was particularly inspired by the health writings of a 19th century female writer Ellen G White.

After 12 years of living in a rainforest, and in a difficult relationship, Barbara left the marriage and moved closer to civilization to allow her older children to obtain work.

Barbara's interest in health knowledge led her to study and obtain a Diploma in Naturopathy in 1994 and later in 2005 as a Nutritionist. Barbara's real healing success springs from the knowledge of the body's ability to heal itself, and then working 'with' the body to achieve the healing response.

After her marriage breakdown in 1993, Barbara put her energies into raising her children and in 1996 moved to Queensland where she worked at Living Valley Springs Health Retreat as a Naturopath. It was here she renewed an old friendship with the Retreat Business Manager Michael O'Neill and they were married in October 1997.

The following year, Barbara and her family of now eight children, (Michael had two children), moved to Narbethong, Victoria where they started a health retreat as a non-profit organization. They continued there for nearly six years, and in 2003 relocated to their new property near Bellbrook, NSW. They then started their new venture, Misty Mountain Health Retreat.

Over the years Barbara has become a highly sought-after health lecturer, as people appreciate her common sense approach to health problems. Barbara's lecture series have circulated around the globe via TV stations, video, DVD, TikTok and YouTube. They have touched the lives of hundreds of thousands of people, and have brought relief to thousands of suffering individuals as they embrace the simple and powerful laws of health.

Currently retired from her role as Health Director of Misty Mountain Lifestyle Retreat, Barbara is now travelling all over the world running seminars on health principles to live a longer, healthier and happier life.

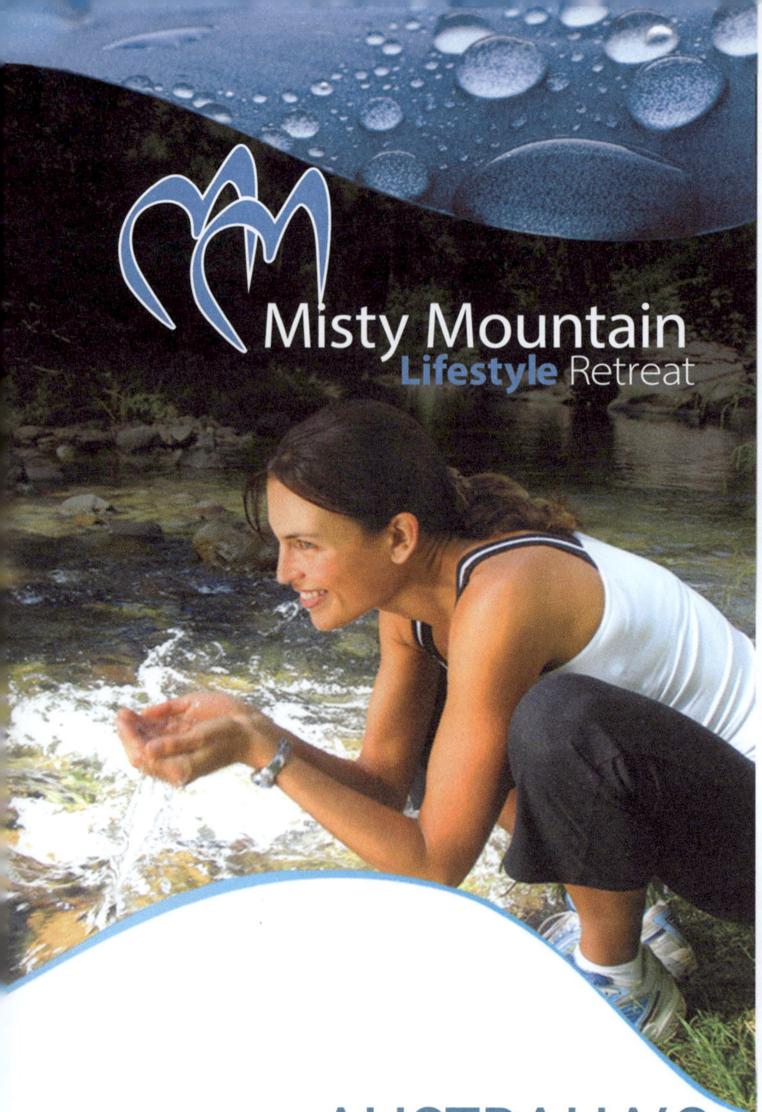
Misty Mountain
Lifestyle Retreat